Adding Cross *to* Crown

Adding Cross *to* Crown

The Political Significance
of Christ's Passion

MARK A. NOLL

with responses by

James D. Bratt
Max L. Stackhouse
James W. Skillen

edited by Luis E. Lugo

The
Center
for Public
Justice
P.O. Box 48368
Washington, D.C. 20002

Baker Books
A Division of Baker Book House Co
Grand Rapids, Michigan 49516

©1996 by The Center for Public Justice

Published by Baker Books
a division of Baker Book House Company
P.O. Box 6287, Grand Rapids, MI 49516-6287

Printed in the United States of America

Library of Congress Cataloging-in-Publication Data

Noll, Mark A., 1946–
    Adding Cross to crown : the political significance of Christ's Passion / Mark A. Noll ; with responses by James D. Bratt, Max L. Stackhouse, and James W. Skillen ; Luis E. Lugo, editor
        p. cm.
    Includes bibliographical references.
    ISBN 0-8010-5731-0 (pbk.)
    1. Christianity and politics. 2. Church and state. 3. Jesus Christ—Person and offices. 4. Jesus Christ—Crucifixion. 5. Jesus Christ—Royal office. I. Bratt, James D., 1949– . II. Stackhouse, Max L. III. Skillen, James W. IV. Lugo, Luis E., 1951– . V. Title.
BR115.P7N595 1996
261.7—dc20   96-22613

Contents

Foreword

Luis E. Lugo

The public way in which religious forces have broken out all over the world has baffled the academic experts and re-opened debates many in the West had long considered settled. In the United States, these public expressions of religious vitality have made it increasingly obvious that a strong commitment to the institutional separation of church and state does not necessarily answer all the questions. It is clear that these religious forces are much too dynamic to be neatly tucked away into a private sphere; they demand public expression beyond the sphere of the church. Very quickly, it seems, the debate has turned from the question of whether religion has a legitimate public role to play to the far more fruitful one of what its appropriate role in the public square truly is. Constitutionally speaking, we could say that the emphasis has shifted from the antiestablishment stipulations of the First Amendment to its guarantee of the free exercise of religion.

Luis E. Lugo (Ph.D., University of Chicago) is Associate Director of the Center for Public Justice and professor of political science at Calvin College. He is the editor of *Religion, Public Life, and the American Polity* (Knoxville: University of Tennessee Press, 1994) and *Sovereignty at the Crossroads? Morality and International Politics in the Post–Cold War Era* (Lanham, Md.: Rowman & Littlefield, 1996).

The Kuyper Lecture series aims to focus attention on the deepest and broadest questions concerning religion and public life. The series takes its name and inspiration from the person and work of Abraham Kuyper (1837–1920), the influential Dutch scholar-statesman whose many contributions to public life were motivated by a desire to offer a creative Christian response to the big questions of faith and politics in the modern world. The lectures do not for the most part focus on Kuyper himself but rather provide an opportunity for thoughtful Christian leaders to bring these matters before a wider public and cast further light on them.

Kuyper was very much aware of the deep, driving influence of competing religions in human society. He also understood that Christ's claims of authority extend to the entire world. That combination logically would seem to lead him straight to a declaration of cultural war against religious adversaries. Kuyper was of the view, however, that the Christian faith could speak meaningfully to this religious diversity, and do so in a noncrusading fashion. He was convinced that a properly oriented Christian politics could make a major contribution toward the creation of a public square where a genuine pluralism, rather than religious warfare, would predominate. It is in the hope of furthering this project that the Center for Public Justice has launched the Kuyper Lectures.

The papers gathered in this volume are the fruit of the inaugural lecture in this series, delivered in the fall of 1995 at Calvin College in Grand Rapids, Michigan. The Center for Public Justice was pleased to be able to cosponsor this first Kuyper Lecture with Calvin College, an academic institution where the influence of the Kuyperian tradition is clearly in evidence. The Center was also pleased to have as the inaugural lecturer Professor Mark Noll, a historian and authority on the role of religion in public life. Noll's long association with the Center and his impressive scholarly contribution to the study of faith and politics made him a natural choice for this task.

In his essay "Adding Cross to Crown: The Political Significance of Christ's Passion," Noll explores what difference it might make for Christian politics to season images of Christ's kingly rule with images of his suffering on the cross. His conclusion is that the difference could be great indeed, especially in helping to nurture a proper attitude toward our political involvement. Noll is of the view that Christ's work on the cross instills the political virtue of humility by reminding us that we are only sinners saved by grace. A consideration of the person of Christ produces a similar benefit, according to Noll. The doubleness of Christ's incarnation—his being fully human and fully God—highlights the elements of contingency and particularity in all our temporal endeavors and thus acts as a powerful inducement to a Christian politics characterized by a healthy sense of moderation.

Noll illustrates his point by making reference to historical examples of Christian political involvement in the United States and elsewhere that stand as sobering reminders of the negative tendency often evident in a so-called Christian politics. As they move closer to political power, Noll observes, Christians can lose their proper christological focus and begin to rely instead on their own self-confidence as they seek to translate Christian convictions into political programs. When that happens, even the symbols associated with the cross can be put to ends far removed from their original meanings. It is for this reason that Noll wants us to consider, as he provocatively puts it, what the leaven of Lutheran cross-centeredness can add to the lump of Calvinist kingly rule.

The crown-cross divide admittedly may present a problem, but does it not also have its virtues? In "Cross, Crown, and Kuyper's Legacy," James Bratt answers in the affirmative, pointing out much more emphatically than Noll the historical abuses, from the time of the Crusades on, of bringing the cross into the public square. According to Bratt, these dangers follow because the symbols associated with the Second Person of the Trinity are by their nature quite specific and thus fail to provide common ground in a religiously diverse polity. One of the strengths of the Kuyperian appeal to the order of creation, Bratt contends, is that it makes possible a more inclusive understanding of the body politic, one that is not tied to any particularistic creed.

There are other reasons why Bratt, despite sharing some of Noll's concerns about crown-theology, is somewhat skeptical of where Noll's argument might lead us. Bratt observes, for example, that historically a politics that takes the incarnation as its orienting focus has tended, as in the Lutheran community, to produce an attitude of political passivity in the face of injustice. When it comes to method, moreover, Bratt agrees with Noll that historical contingency plays a crucial role in politics and that principles do not operate in the abstract, but he also worries that an emphasis on particularity can easily lead to a kind of pragmatism that is all too willing to cloak its meanest interests with the mantle of practicality. These reservations notwithstanding, Bratt concludes by stating that if no other observation in Noll's essay has theological warrant, this one surely does: No political theory, however rigorously constructed, will relieve our need for judgment and for discerning the movement of the times.

In "Public Theology and Christological Politics," Max Stackhouse shifts the focus from history to theology and raises important questions about Noll's argument. Stackhouse questions whether Noll emphasizes Christology at the expense of a more rigorous trinitarian approach, one that brings the person and work of Christ into a dynamic relationship with the other Persons of the Godhead. Only when we give the Trinity priority over Christology, Stackhouse argues, will we be able to achieve a proper understanding of the diversified nature of covenant and office. This in turn will help us resist the temptation to reduce

Christian politics to a highly personal, ultimately exclusive particularism where the attitudes of converted individuals serve as the main link between Christ and politics.

Stackhouse sees other benefits as well in a trinitarian approach. These include a strengthened sense of the plural nature of civil society, of its priority over politics, and of the varied nature of the church's ongoing influence on society. This last point is especially important for Stackhouse, and he devotes the final section of his paper to it. His main observation here is that the church's engagement in politics is indirect rather than through an immediate seizing of political power. He points out that for Christians this means our involvement is necessarily mediated by a public philosophy and by practical wisdom. The indirect way in which Christians work in politics, and not some false piety that hides a reluctance to speak with clarity on public issues, is the real source of that humility Noll rightly believes ought to accompany all Christian political involvement.

In a concluding essay, "Where Kingdom Politics Should Lead Us," James Skillen joins the conversation and offers some observations on how the discussion touches on the central themes of the Kuyper Lecture series and the work of the Center for Public Justice. Skillen affirms Noll's desire to counteract mistaken appropriations of Christ's kingly rule, but he wonders whether both Noll and Bratt have not allowed a certain Christian triumphalism and messianic self-righteousness to stand as the necessary expression of crown-theology. Even more serious are Skillen's reservations about placing the cross in tension with the crown as a way to get at the problem. He suggests that we seek instead to recapture a broader covenantal context where crown and cross, creation and redemption, are seen in their true meaning and proper connection. Politically speaking, Skillen contends, the cross of Christ does not stand in dialectical relation to his crown; rather, the cross seals the death of all contradictions against creation and signals its complete restoration.

Skillen also questions whether humility is sufficient to define a Christian approach to politics. Whether generated by a sense of our own sinfulness, by a realization that we of ourselves cannot bring in the fullness of Christ's kingdom, or simply by a sense of our creaturely limitations, an attitude of humility will do little, according to Skillen, to clarify for us the nature of the political order and of our civic responsibility within it. Here he believes the admonitions of Stackhouse about a structurally diverse society are more to the point, for political humility properly understood means bowing before God's real intentions for creation, and working politically for a political order that extends legal recognition to the various spheres of society. In contrast to Stackhouse, however, Skillen is of the view that the connection between Christ and politics is much more direct and not solely mediated through the church.

The exchange among our authors does not, of course, settle all the issues touching on the proper relationship of cross to crown for thinking clearly and acting responsibly as Christian citizens. It does, however, serve to underscore the great importance all of us should attach to the task of basing our politics on sound biblical principles. Noll's thought-provoking essay and the theologically and historically informed comments of the respondents provide us with an excellent starting point for such a reflection. By setting a serious and respectful tone for discussion of the big questions about religion and public life, they also set a high standard for the Kuyper Lecture series.

To receive the twelve-page booklet introducing the Kuyper Lecture series or to rent or purchase a video cassette copy of the inaugural Kuyper Lecture, please write to the Center for Public Justice, P.O. Box 48368, Washington, D.C. 20002.

Introduction

Is there diadem as Monarch,
That his brow adorns?
Yea, a crown, in very surety,
But of thorns.

John Mason Neale (1862)

I want to explore the difference it could make for Christians to concentrate on the person and work of Christ when they think about the nature of politics or when they engage in political activity. Specifically Christian efforts in political thought and practice have historically featured biblical themes of divine creation, human fallenness, God-given human capacity, the kingly rule of Christ, and the restoration of creation. Such efforts have often been extraordinarily beneficial; I do not think they should be replaced. But perhaps they can be supplemented, deepened, and broadened by specific attention to the redemptive work of Christ.

Because God is integral and because every aspect of God's revelation to humanity flows from divine integrity, Christian dogma should also be integral—its various pieces should depend upon each other. Christian soteriology traditionally has featured human sinfulness, the work of Christ on the cross, and the saving ministry of the Holy Spirit. But in order to grasp the significance of these realities, it is necessary also to see them in relationship to general considerations of creation, the church, divinely ordained ideals for social relationships, and the kingly rule of Christ. In the same way, when seeking to formulate principles for Christian politics, it is entirely appropriate to feature considerations of humanity in general as created by God and ruled by God, but these matters also deserve to be considered in light of how God redeems the elect.

At this point it is necessary to proceed cautiously. When we speak of Christ and his work, we must not identify Christ only with the cross, the resurrection, and the redemption of God's people. Jesus Christ is the Redeemer, but the same Jesus Christ is also the incarnate Son of God, the Second Person of the Trinity, through whom and for whom all things were created in the beginning and in whom all things will at the last day be offered humbly to the Father. The point in urging fuller consideration of the specifically soteriological aspects of Christ and his work is not to contrast a suffering and redeeming Christ with an otherwise natural order of reason, natural revelation, and the general providence of God the Father. Rather, the point is to heighten our sense of the ineluctably organic harmony among creation, judgment, redemption, and eschatological fulfillment. A plea to focus attention on the redeeming Christ is not, therefore, an appeal to neglect or deny the creating Christ, the ruling Christ, or the eschatological Christ. It is, rather, an appeal to seek the resplendent plenitude of Christ and his work, and so to err neither on the side of a world-denying pietism or a redemption-denying immanentism.[1]

Those Christians who confess that Christ and his work must have a this-worldly significance along with its otherworldly significance are precisely the believers best situated to consider Christian soteriology in connection with politics, since they will not be tempted to swing to the extreme of an otherworldly piety. At the same time, however, it is important for Christians of whatever sort to consider the ways that soteriology is foundational to human relations with God. In order to be more faithful to the character of

Christianity itself, in other words, efforts to formulate a Christian politics may well need to supplement consideration of God as creator with consideration of God as trinitarian redeemer. To images of the believer as saint ruling alongside of Christ must be added images of the believer as sinner redeemed solely by the grace of God in Christ. Alongside the general principles of God's written Word, a Christian politics should also heed closely what is written about the Word made flesh. In other words, when thinking about politics, it is worth considering what the leaven of Lutheran cross-centeredness can add to an already nutritious lump of Calvinist kingly rule.[2] Put most simply, I want to explore the difference it might make if Christian politics featured Christ.

The effort to think like a Christian about politics is a worthy task for believers in all times and places, but it is an especially important task today. In the United States, we are witnessing a resurgence of explicitly Christian political action unlike anything seen in this country since the years before the Civil War when several political parties with distinct Christian aspirations made their mark on the national scene. Whether groups like the Christian Coalition live up to their name as "Christian" is, of course, an important question,[3] but no one can deny the importance of the Coalition, or of other centers of Christian political involvement found among Catholics, Protestants, and in alliances transcending even the historic division between Catholics and Protestants.[4] In Canada the Reform Party, which burst on the national scene with surprising success in that country's last federal election, features a more explicit link to specifically Christian concerns than has any Canadian political body since the rise of Social Credit and the Cooperative Commonwealth Federation over fifty years ago.[5]

Elsewhere around the world Christian concerns are now more visible than anyone could ever have thought possible even a decade ago. Whether one thinks of the political awakening of the huge Zionist churches in South Africa, behind-the-scenes efforts to bridge Catholic-Protestant divisions in

Northern Ireland, the apocalyptic fears of Norwegian pietists concerning the European Union, the reawakening of Orthodox political aspirations in Eastern Europe and the former Soviet Union, the political role of Pentecostals in selected Latin American countries, the influence of a reforming Catholicism in other Latin regions, the surprising contribution of Christians to the struggle for Palestinian liberation, or the lucid assessments of political realities from the current pope—the world is witnessing a remarkable resurgence of Christian political activity. At such a moment, an effort to think about the significance for politics of the person and work of Christ is as timely as it is important.

This essay begins with the general argument that apprehension of the person and work of Christ, within the context of the Trinity, is inescapably the starting point for all Christian reflection, including Christian reflection on politics. It then goes on to suggest that for neglecting the bearing of Christology on politics, the practice of Christian politics in America and elsewhere has often fallen short of Christian ideals. It closes with suggestions for how concentration on a fuller range of christological realities, especially the meaning of the incarnation, may improve attitudes in political situations as well as theorizing about the nature of politics.[6]

1

Christ and Christian Reflection on Politics

Creation-Based Politics

In the eye of God, creation comes first, then fall, then redemption, then at the end the restoration of all things. Christian politics is often, and profitably, constructed by following reality as God experiences reality. So perceived, the creation of humanity includes a potential for political life that, if pursued faithfully and if the effects of the fall are checked, contributes to human flourishing. In these terms, the potential for a just political order is one of the many gifts of God bestowed upon all humanity in the creation. The Christian's task is to follow the trajectory of creation and work toward a fulfillment of the political good that God originally intended and continues, by his providence, to make possible. In this picture, sin and its effects, as well as grace and its effects, can be taken quite seriously, for sin counteracts the potential for good that God made possible in creation, while grace enables the repentant sinner to promote political justice as one way of serving God. In this view,

Christian politics is primarily an effort to realize the potential built into the creation and to serve God by doing his will in the political sphere.

The great virtues of this approach, considered very generally, have been exemplified in various ways by the Thomistic tradition, John Calvin, John Knox and the Scottish reformers, the English and American Puritans, Guillaume Groen van Prinsterer, Abraham Kuyper, twentieth-century neo-Calvinists, and modern neo-Thomists. What these people and movements share is a desire to employ God's own vision as displayed in a perfect creation, and in what God has revealed about the eschatological restoration of that creation, in order to forge an understanding of politics and to shape an agenda for political practice. The virtues inherent in this approach have been most apparent when its proponents practice politics as part of what the Heidelberg Catechism calls the "gratitude I owe to God for . . . redemption."

The Need for Humility

I find no problem with this general approach, as such, if only those who formulate a Christian politics on the basis of creation and the restoration of creation remember who they are. Christians, that is, should never forget that they are not God. Rather, it is a central teaching of their religion to remember that they are sinners saved by grace. Moreover, they are saved by God's grace as fully displayed in the incarnate Christ. And the incarnate Christ, in the classic formula of Chalcedon, is at once fully God and fully human—"this one and the same Christ . . . made known in two natures." Each of these realities is directly or indirectly an aspect of Christology. Each is also big with implications for the understanding and practice of politics.

Believers know that they are not God. Nowhere is this knowledge sharper than when Christians are measured against the command of Christ to be perfect as the Father in heaven is perfect (Matt. 5:48). That is, believers realize most concretely their separateness from God when they see themselves most clearly as sinners and realize most keenly their need of the Savior. In fact, until we see ourselves as sinners in need of a savior, it is doubtful if we see anything clearly at all. Philosophers and theologians debate the noetic effects of the fall—the toll that our fallen condition takes on our ability to see ourselves, the world, and God clearly.[1] And well they should, for the persistent tendency of unbelief is to treat the self, or sometimes one's group, as if it were God and thereby to lose perspective on all things—on God, on self, on our group, and on the world besides. To be a Christian is to confess, joyfully, that God is God and I am not.

The leaven that this soteriological reality adds to the political lump is the reminder that however much God may be a supralapsarian, all humans experience life as infralapsarians. However much God may have made possible the good potential for politics before humanity fell into sin, all humans experience the creation from their position as persons who are alienated by sin from God. The implication must be that when Christians define the potential for politics as rooted in divine creation and pointed toward eschatological fulfillment, they do so with the awareness that their grasp of politics remains the grasp of a creature graciously granted partial insight into the purposes of God. Human knowledge, even redeemed human knowledge, can never be divine in its fullness, its purity, and its perfection. Accordingly, for Christians who know that they are saved by grace, there will be no political judgments rendered as if from Mount Sinai, there will be no pronouncement of doom on political opponents, and there will be no promise of paradise for choosing a particular political path—since judgments of Sinai, pronouncements of doom, and promises of paradise are powers reserved to God alone.

A similar benefit arises for Christian politics when believers continually remind themselves that not only are we not God but we are also sinners saved by grace. The category distinction is simple but profound in its effects. At the start, in the middle, and at the end of a Christian's pilgrimage, the Christian is reconciled to God and the purposes of God by God alone and never because of our own perfection. The implications for politics of this realism, this recognition that perfection awaits the life to come, are as simple as they are elusive. A properly Christian politics will display humility, a willingness to question one's own motives, and the expectation that reform of political vision will always be needed because even Christian politics is carried out by individuals who know they are still sinners, however glad they are to be sinners saved by grace.

The Incarnation and Political Thinking

It makes a more subtle, but no less important, political difference to realize that the means of our redemption, and the reason why we know that we are not God and that we are sinners saved by grace, is the incarnation of God the Son. If our entire apprehension of the world is shaped by our need of a savior, and if God offers himself as that savior, then the means by which God offers the savior should affect our apprehension of the entire world, including the world of politics.

For the purposes of political reflection, one of the most striking things about the incarnation is its miraculous combination of the particular and the universal. The nature of that miraculous combination, as well as hints about the political implications of that combination, have been put well by the Scottish missiologist Andrew Walls: "Christ took flesh and was made man in a particular time and place, family, nationality, tradition and customs and sanctified them, while still being for all men in every time and place.

Wherever he is taken by the people of any day, time and place, he sanctifies that culture—he is living in it. And no other group of Christians has any right to impose in his name a set of assumptions about life determined by another time and place. But to acknowledge this is not to forget that there is another, and equally important, force at work among us. Not only does God in His mercy take people as they are: He takes them to transform them into what He wants them to be."[2] To extrapolate Walls's insight more specifically for political purposes, the nature of the incarnation suggests that a fully Christian politics will incorporate the full weight of contingent circumstances, developments, and events in particular cultures as well as the general truths of the Christian revelation.

Believers who see the way in which the incarnation both dignifies particular cultures and brings a universal saving truth may expect, for example, that political justice in the new Republic of South Africa will incorporate aspects of traditional tribal hierarchicalism as well as aspects of Western democratic capitalism. Those who promote the spread of justice in relations between church and state for the rapidly changing nations of Eastern Europe might expect to find aspects of the region's historic Caesaropapism functioning with, instead of simply standing in opposition to, properly universal ideals of religious liberty.

Americans concerned about opportunities for Christian values in public life may well learn a lesson from Canadian experience where, for at least much of this century and at least in comparison with the United States, citizens have been less preoccupied with grand national strategies and more concerned about working out procedures for education, health care, and labor legislation at provincial and local levels. The result is much less uniformity in Canadian public life as a whole. Newfoundland, for example, has funded its primary and secondary public education through a system of church-sponsored schools while some western provinces provide tuition payment but not capital investment to sectarian schools. But also by comparison with the United States, in the Canadian situation we find a better balance between particular local circumstances and broad national standards. It is too crass to say that the Canadian pattern embodies christological realities where the United States does not, but not extreme to say that in this one instance the structure of Canadian political life tends more in the direction of the combination of particular and universal embodied in the incarnation than does American political life.

If it is valuable to let the incarnation's combination of local reality and universal truth shape Christian political expectation, so too might it be possible to allow reflection on the very character of the incarnation itself to influence our thinking, including thinking about politics. Such reflection, however, can be disconcerting, for it features the well-known doubleness of classical christological dogma—that Jesus Christ was fully God, fully human, and though fully human and divine, one integral human being. The reality of this dogma as well as the difficulty in relating its tension has been well sketched recently by the theologian Gabriel Fackre, who in recommending the work of Søren Kierkegaard, Sergius Bulgakov, and Donald Baillie has shown how their writing "pointed to antinomies all over scripture and Christian teaching, paradigmatically in the doctrine of the incarnation, and it noted that the assertion of mutually exclusive propositions—humanity and divinity in one person—never satisfies human reason, which is always interested in relaxing the tension in one direction or the other."[3]

The political point from such realizations—that a fully orthodox view of Christ affirms a doubleness with which human reason has been historically uncomfortable—is that we should not be surprised to find a corresponding doubleness in political life. If, that is, the incarnation stands at the heart of reality, or at least reality as perceived by sinners saved by grace, then perhaps political reality may display a doubleness hard to fathom by conventional human categories. We might conclude, therefore, with an eye toward the incarnate Christ positioned at the very heart of the universe, that many of our political judgments should be as complex as we can possibly make them. For example, that for preserving a constitutional system through the Great Depression and the Second World War, Franklin D. Roosevelt was one of our greatest presidents, but also for expanding nearly without limit the power of government over against other God-given spheres of authority, FDR was at exactly the same time one of our worst presidents. If the heart of our religion affirms the cosmic significance of a single person who is fully divine and fully human, and if we affirm that our religion shapes our entire view of the world, then such odd conjunctions of apparently contradictory realities can only be expected in politics as in other spheres of life.

The Seasoning of Christ's Suffering

In sum, I am suggesting that because our need for salvation is central to our lives, it should be central also to our perception of the world, including the political world. Since the means of redemption is an incarnation that legitimates both cultural particularity and universal absolutes, so ought a Christian politics make room for local particularities alongside universal absolutes. Finally, since the incarnate Christ stands at the center of existence as humans must perceive that existence, since the incarnate Christ is central for the life of every Christian, and since the incarnation embodies the miraculous fact of divine and human natures joined in one person "without confusion, without change, without division, and without separation," so might we expect in every human sphere—including politics—to confront situations where two apparently different, or even contradictory, things are present indissolubly in one actual reality.

Reflection on creation and the restoration of creation has been a rich source for the construction of Christian political thought and action. In proposing to enlist Christology directly for politics, I do not see the need to abandon any of the achievements gained by concentrating on creation and its restoration. It may be, however, that those who quite properly exploit the God-given realities of created political potential will do so even more fully, and with more occasion to praise the name of God, by seasoning images of Christ's ruling at the head of the saints over a restored creation with images of Christ's suffering for the saints on the cross.

2

Christology
and the Practice of Politics

The Cross-Power Conundrum

The practical importance of the cross for politics can be illustrated in the history of almost any place on the globe where Christians have constituted a large enough group to exert real political influence. In those situations where Christians either have exercised power or have had a history of exercising power, the implications for a politics of the cross are often set aside in favor of a vision of a restored creation ruled over by Christ and the saints. By contrast, when believers have constituted distinct minorities in their nations or cultures, they have not needed to be instructed about the importance of the cross. Theocracy, in other words, is usually not an option where no opportunity exists to exercise power. The importance of the cross, by contrast, may be greatest precisely in those times and places where believers have had the most chance to exercise power. Such chances have included many venues in the Christian Middle Ages, many situations in the Orthodox regions of central and eastern Europe, most of the European nations in the immediate wake of the Reformation and the Counter-Reformation, and much of the history played out over the last few centuries in the United States and Canada.

What these situations reveal is a conundrum. Christian life focused around the cross is a motive force that propels churches and their adherents into dominant political positions, but once in dominant positions, their politics usually features themes of righteousness, holiness, and commandment-keeping more closely associated with doctrines of a restored creation rather than the themes of humility, self-abasement, and repentance associated with the cross. To put complicated historical situations much too crudely, there would have been no opportunity for the political influence of Constantinianism in the fourth century if there had not existed remarkable success in proclaiming the new message of a crucified God throughout the Mediterranean world of the second and third centuries. There would have been no rise of an imperial papacy in the twelfth and thirteenth centuries if there had not been a movement of monastic renewal energized by meditations like Bernard of Clairvaux's on the sacred head of Christ now wounded. There would have been no Protestant regimes in sixteenth-century Europe if it had not been for the effective proclamation to unworthy sinners of justification by free grace, nor would there have been a neo-Calvinist Christian democratic movement in the Netherlands if leaders like Abraham Kuyper had not been overwhelmed by experiences of God's grace.

Coming closer to our North American experience, there would have been no thought of setting up the kingly rule of Christ in Scotland had not John Knox and his colleagues so effectively proclaimed the authority of the crucified Christ. There would have been no attempt at Puritan hegemony under Oliver Cromwell in England and no successful establishment of a Puritan way of life in New England if there had not been several generations of effective Puritan preachers who knew how to call wounded consciences to the Great Shepherd. There would have been no effort in nineteenth-century Protestant America to protect the nation from Roman Catholics, southern Europeans, Asians, and other "aliens" if earnest evangelical preachers had not so successfully proclaimed in towns, villages, and fields the message of a merciful savior. There would have been no biblical defense of a "Southern way of life" in the decades before the Civil War if multitudes of Southerners had not found forgiveness for their sin through the biblical message of Christ. There would have been no aspiration in nineteenth-century Canada to the status of "His Dominion from sea to sea" had not several generations of Canadian evangelists called their fellows to the self-denial of conversion. And one presumes there would be no Christian Coalition today if masses of ordinary Americans had not experienced what the pollsters call a "born-again experience" or an "intense religious experience focused on the person of Jesus Christ." Historically considered, in sum, the effort to mount an effective Christian politics—the effort to guide society in the kingly name of Christ—has been unthinkable without a prior commitment to the work of Christ on the cross.

Yet once aspiring to make a difference in the political sphere, once set on a course of defending or propagating a vision of reality generated by an experience of the suffering Christ, believers regularly push the consideration of Christ's two natures, of his suffering and of his redeeming work, to the side. Righteousness rather than forgiveness, and duty rather than repentance become the watchwords. To be sure, this posture is by no means entirely misguided. It is a political analogy to the pilgrimage of the individual believer from regeneration and conversion through sanctification toward glorification. But just as the redeeming work of Christ remains important for the proper outworking of sanctification, so too the cross of Christ should remain important for the ones who, having been redeemed, make an attempt to rule in Christ's name.

The memory of realities associated with the cross unfortunately has usually faded rapidly in American experience once believers turn their direct attention from what constitutes them as Christians to what needs to be done politically. So it certainly was in the decades before the Civil War with the Anti-Masonic, Liberty, and American (or Know-Nothing) political parties. Christian belief and energy contributed substantially to the creation of each of these parties. Christian zeal was responsible for the remarkable, if short lived, success each of them enjoyed. The organizers of these Christian political parties had grasped firmly the intensity of the mandate to make the kingdoms of this world into the kingdom of our Lord and of his Christ. But they missed the reality that they were themselves redeemed by the Lord of creation, that the political opponents whom they demonized were individuals for whom Christ died, and that none of the defining issues around which they organized were as clear cut as they thought. Evaluated in Christian terms that embrace both cross and crown, those Christian political parties were half right, and therefore doubly dangerous. They took seriously the need to exalt Christian standards in the political world, but they erred grievously by assuming that they had moved beyond the need of the cross and in so doing may have damaged the cause of Christianity itself.

Christological Themes in American Politics

Christological themes have regularly played a major role in the mainstream of American political life. In fact, two of the most dramatic pronouncements in all of American political rhetoric exploited powerful references to Christ. When William Jennings Bryan addressed the Democratic National Convention in Chicago during its platform debate in 1896, he was still a political stripling who had not lost any of his idealism by serving in Congress or as a newspaper editor in Omaha. His rousing address attacked efforts to keep gold as the only support of United States currency even as it urged, as a way of helping debtor farmers and small-scale entrepreneurs, the free coinage of silver. Bryan's reference to christological realities in the peroration of his speech was as dramatic as it could be: "If they dare to come out in the open field and defend the gold standard as a good thing, we will fight them to the uttermost. Having behind us the producing masses of this nation and the world, supported by the commercial interests, the laboring interests, and the toilers everywhere, we will answer their demand for a gold standard by saying to them: You shall not press down upon the brow of labor this crown of thorns, you shall not crucify mankind upon a cross of gold."[1]

Only sixteen years later in 1912, again in Chicago, another crusading idealist also enlisted a christological image as the concluding metaphor for a powerful political oration. On June 17, the very day that the Republican National Convention chose William Howard Taft as its presidential nominee over Theodore Roosevelt, Roosevelt responded with a stem-winding speech to his supporters. In this address Roosevelt pledged himself to a no-holds-barred fight against the knavery of political bosses and the corruption of crooked businessmen. He ended with these words: "We fight in honorable fashion for the good of mankind; fearless of the future; unheeding of our individual fates; with unflinching hearts and undimmed eyes; we stand at Armageddon, and we battle for the Lord."[2]

A comparison of these two speeches is instructive. Theodore Roosevelt employed the language of the ruling Christ leading his faithful followers into battle against a well-defined foe. Unlike Roosevelt, Bryan employed the language of the cross, but like Roosevelt, Bryan used christological language to inspire supporters for a fight against the hosts of wickedness that threatened him and his fellow saints from without. This use of cross-language in the same militant manner as crown-language is far from uncommon in Western history. The most important precedent was the Crusades, where believers "took the cross" as a symbol of their desire to push Islam out of the Holy Land.

Bryan's use of the cross as a symbol inspiring a crusade against an external foe is by no means rare in the American experience. The two best-known hymns surviving from the era of the Civil War, for example, both employ Christology to these ends. The Presbyterian minister George Duffield wrote "Stand up, stand up for Jesus! Ye soldiers of the cross" in the heat of revival in 1858, but it became a much-beloved hymn in the Union army.[3] The best-known anthem of the Civil War itself, "The Battle Hymn of the Republic," written by Unitarian Julia Ward Howe, raised the employment of gospel- or cross-focused language to a high art. The hymn not only linked Christ's birth "in the beauty of the lilies" with the need for dying "to make men free," it also jumbled gospel and self-exertion, grace and works, spiritual tyranny and temporal tyranny, with breathtaking abandon, as is well illustrated in one of the hymn's later verses:

> I have read a fiery gospel writ in burnish'd rows of steel;
> "As ye deal with my condemners, so with you my grace
>   shall deal!"
> Let the hero, born of women, crush the serpent with his
>   heel,
> Since God is marching on.

One contemporary reference illustrates the way that Christology continues to be put to use in this combative style. Following the defeat in November 1994 of a Florida referendum that would have expanded casino gambling in that state, a leader of the antigambling forces was quoted as saying that when it comes to gambling, "the ballot box is like the cross to Dracula."[4]

These christological references share a common form. The one who employs the image is beset by sinister foes. Images from the story of Jesus are presumed to resonate with sacred power. The speaker identifies himself or herself with Christ's own struggle against the hosts of evil. Christological images link the speaker's viewpoint with the righteousness of Christ. So connected, the speaker and the speaker's cause share, at least rhetorically, the supreme sacred power evoked by the christological image.

Regarded theologically, the use of these images is problematic. In classical theology, Christ does manifest great power—defeating sin, death, and the devil while establishing the church as an institution eternally secure against its raging foes. But it is the means by which Christ exercises his power that makes christological rhetoric a curious motif in American political battles. In the gospels, Jesus says that "the Son of Man came . . . to give his life" (Matt. 20:28). He said that God the Son had no place by night to lay his head (Matt. 8:20). In the climactic hour of his earthly existence, Jesus rebuked those who would fight on his behalf. In the great hymn of Philippians chapter two, Christ at his incarnation gives up the prerogatives of deity and assumes the inauspicious form of an ordinary servant. In the New Testament, as opposed to American political rhetoric, Jesus accepts a crown of thorns and also welcomes the agonizing shame of the cross. Christ indeed promises to appear in the last day with power and great glory, but only in the last day. In the interim, in anticipation of that last day, those who would be Christians are urged to take up their crosses and follow Jesus—not to victory, but to the denial of their own selves. If, therefore, we follow the christological metaphors used by Christians in American politics back to their source, if in particular we value the cross as the cross is valued in Scripture, it is hard to recognize this combative American Christology as anything but a perversion.

The Effects of the Cross

My point is not a radical one. I do not hold that all believers must imitate literally the self-abnegating Christ nor so concentrate on the passive repentance required for justifying grace as to abandon the political sphere. Such radicalism flows from an artificial pietism that seriously unbalances the biblical account of Jesus and his work. The suffering Savior is, in fact, also the ruling Son. The kingdom that must be entered as a child offers full and satisfying work for adults. The point, rather, is that the sort of Christian politics we have seen so often in America, but not only in America, should more accurately be styled "so-called Christian politics." A Christian politics that forgets the cross, a Christian politics that neglects the realities of redemption, a Christian politics that assumes a godlike stance toward the world, is a Christian politics that has abandoned Christ.

But what would a Christian politics look like that remembered Christ, that recalled the cross with the crown, that kept in mind the realities of justification while going on to the tasks of sanctification? I suspect that from the outside, a politics that is Christian in this sense would not look too different from responsible political action advanced by, say, Catholics or Calvinists. It would be a politics attempting to discover for any specific problem or in any general situation the path of justice and the appropriately just means to advance the cause of justice.

To be sure, a Christ-centered politics would feature the themes that loom large in the Scriptures that Christ taught, recommended, and embodied. Themes like the necessity for rulers to act fairly or like the need to protect those who cannot protect themselves are so richly displayed in the entirety of Scripture as in the work of Christ himself that it is reasonable to expect these themes to be prominent in any truly Christian politics. By the same standard of biblical norms, a truly Christian politics will also tend to concentrate much more diligently on the rights of others than on one's own rights.[5] But within such basic biblical guidelines, the practicalities of a Christian politics alert to the cross may not differ all that much from a Christian politics inspired by the vision of the ruling Christ. Where awareness of the cross, and the circle of redemptive realities for which it stands, may make more of a difference, however, is in the attitudes we carry into the political fray and in the perspectives we hold on the nature of politics itself.

3

Christian Attitudes toward Politics

The Attitudes of Various Traditions

Attitudes—mental and emotional expectations, levels and qualities of commitments, judgments of self and others—must, by the nature of the case, be strongly influenced by our view of Christ. To put the historical situation in very general terms, Christian approaches to politics within four of the most important Christian traditions can be said to be marked by relatively straightforward attitudes. In their own way, Orthodox, Roman Catholic, Calvinist, and Anabaptist politics have involved relatively straightforward efforts to define, and then to preserve as under God, the political good. Orthodox, Roman Catholics, Calvinists, and Anabaptists have, of course, differed with each other and among themselves as to what political goals are most important and how they should be preserved. But they have resembled each other in the forthright, clear, and often courageous way they have defined and pursued as Christians the political ends that their visions of the faith spell out.

The Lutheran perspective is different. The Lutheran perspective is marked, as James Nuechterlein has recently put it, by its "dialectic theological framework." As Nuechterlein explains what he means by Lutheran dialectics, we begin to see why a Lutheran perspective cannot foster the straightforward approaches to political matters that, by contrast, are more commonly found among Orthodox, Roman Catholics, Calvinists, and Anabaptists. "The Lutheran dialectic," according to Nuechterlein, "takes a variety of forms: the emphasis on the Law/Gospel distinction as hermeneutical principle and theological guide; the understanding of social ethics and responsibilities according to the doctrine of the Two Kingdoms; the conception of the human condition as essentially *Simul*—we are at once, Luther insisted, sinners and saints, enemies of God and yet fully redeemed participants in His eternal glory."

Not everyone will agree with Nuechterlein that "these distinctly Lutheran perspectives . . . command attention because they conform to the reality of our lives." Yet within other major Christian traditions, believers are aware of how difficult it can be to systematize the different aspects of biblical revelation and how much inner conflict can arise in living out the various dimensions of Christ-centered faith. And so even if others cannot agree with Nuechterlein's judgment about the Lutheran theological difference, they know what experiences he is talking about when he claims that the Lutheran dialectics "fit the rough contrariness of our experience; they are at once contradictory and true. We yearn to be followers of God even as we rebel against His injunctions. The Lutheran *Simul* captures our reality better than do visions of perfection or divinization or anticipation of the eschaton. Lutheranism engages us in our doubled condition and reminds us of its founder's central insight, confessed as he died, that we are all beggars before God. . . . [I]t is within the Lutheran tradition that the antinomies of the faith have been most vibrantly kept alive."[1]

Again, my concern is not with an evaluation of Lutheranism per se as it is with the great value a Lutheran leaven might bring to political reasoning rooted in other theological traditions. Indeed, political history since the Reformation suggests that if left to itself, the Lutheran leaven can sometimes decay into political passivity or encourage an otherworldly pietism that makes very little contribution to living out the gospel in the world.[2] The point, rather, is to suggest that other Christian traditions that encourage a more straightforward, conclusive political thinking and more self-confidently direct political action would benefit from *adding* an element of Lutheran dialectic to the politics derived from their own theologies.

The Lutheran Leaven

How might the Lutheran leaven, proceeding from a concentrated focus on the person and work of Christ, refine the attitudes of Christians active in politics? Two examples must suffice. Luther taught that the essence of the church was to proclaim in word, sacrament, and other visible signs the free grace of God communicated through Jesus Christ. This conviction drove his criticism of the Roman Catholic church of his day, because he thought that the papal system was concentrating on itself instead of pursuing its proper work, which was to convey the message of the forgiveness of sin. Luther's view of the church is similar to that which grounds the assertion of the non-Lutheran New Testament scholar C. K. Barrett that "the church had and has an impossible task, for it can affirm itself only at the cost of denying its own proper being."[3] That is, for the church to defend itself, however legitimately, is to threaten to turn attention away from its most basic role of proclaiming Christ and the free offer of the gospel.

Now consider the debate which certainly must soon arise in our aggressively antitax Congress over income tax deductions for charitable contributions. I happen to think that there are sound reasons for maintaining these deductions—for example, that they play an important role in promoting social justice and the general stability of the body politic—and I hope my opinions find effective advocates when the debate over tax deductible contributions begins. But I also happen to think that a Christian who remembers the potential danger to the gospel when churches begin to assert their own rights will mount a defense of the deduction with a different attitude toward the issue itself and toward those who argue on the other side than a Christian who forgets this foundational christological conviction about the church.

For another example we turn to one of Luther's most enduring contributions in general—his obsessive focus on justification by faith. Regardless of how other believers evaluate his final conclusions on this doctrine, it is possible for all Christians to benefit from Luther's probing of the disguises assumed by works-righteousness. He is also worth heeding when he describes the multifaceted temptations to self-salvation found in human history. Even those who reject Luther's formulation of *sola fide* are better off in the exposition of their own faith for having followed Luther in exposing the multitudinous ways in which humans attempt to save themselves.[4]

Now consider the fight against abortion on demand. I happen to consider this fight the noblest cause of the New Christian Right and the feature of contemporary Christian politics that comes closest to fulfilling the biblical mandate to care for the powerless. While I do not agree with every tactical move or intellectual argument of the most visible pro-life leaders, I commend their work in general and often ask myself why I am not more active on behalf of expectant mothers and their children in utero. But I also happen to think that as vitally important as the pro-life cause is, it is possible that those who sin in promoting abortion may yet be saved by God's free grace in Christ, and that it is possible

for pro-life advocates so thoroughly to commit themselves
to their cause that they run the risk of trusting in their own
pro-life advocacy as the *sine qua non* of their acceptance
before God. I hope a fervent pro-life advocacy that deals
justly with both mothers- and children-to-be will flourish,
but I also hold that the political attitudes of those who think
as I do will be more thoroughly Christian if we continue to
remember that we are pro-life because we are Christians
and not Christians because we are pro-life.

In general, the Lutheran leaven will have its greatest impact in moderating Christian political attitudes in situations
of conflict. There are, and always will be, culture wars. There
are, and always will be, saints defending the truth and
scoffers assaulting the truth. But for one who truly knows
Christ, the culture wars will always be recognized for what
they are—as relatively important battles fought with relatively secure knowledge of who the enemy is and what the
issues at stake are. The reason why the Christian who remembers Christ knows that culture wars can never be
fought with more than relative certainty is spelled out with
piercing clarity by Alexander Solzhenitsyn in *The Gulag
Archipelago* when he writes, "If only [the struggle between
good and evil] were so simple! If only there were evil people
somewhere insidiously committing evil deeds, and it were
necessary only to separate them from the rest of us and de-
stroy them. But the line dividing good and evil cuts through
the heart of every human being. And who is willing to de-
stroy a piece of his own heart?"[5] In a word, there is a field of
combat even more fundamental than the arena of public
culture. That more fundamental field is the human heart
where for every person, believer and unbeliever alike, the
battle between God and self, light and darkness, righteousness and corruption, is fought every day, and where there
will be no absolute, complete, or perfect triumph until the
end of time.

Lutherans are far from the only Christians who realize
how much christological realities should shape the atti-

tudes, including the political attitudes, of believers. It is necessary to think only of Saint Patrick, Bernard of Clairvaux, Francis of Assisi, Blaise Pascal, John Newton, P. T. Forsyth, or John Stott, to name only a few non-Lutherans who have broadcast this truth. At the same time, the striking community of witness that extends from Luther along different lines to Spener and Zinzendorf, to Bach, to Kierkegaard, and to Bonhoeffer is a community testifying eloquently to how a Christian perception of the world will be different, and different for the better, if the suffering, atoning Christ is kept in view.

4

Christian Perspectives on Politics

The Particular and the Incarnation

Much of the best Christian thinking over the centuries on the nature of politics has tended to be theoretical, doctrinal, and aprioristic rather than practical, historical, and contingent. It has arisen more from the universal, permanent relationships God established with the world through creation and by reference to the unchangeableness of his own character than from the contingent, particularized work of the incarnation. Yet concentration on the incarnate Christ shows clearly how vital it is to reason about both God's relationship to humanity and to the hope for human salvation in terms of local conditions, contingent events, particular circumstances, and individual actions.

The ways in which the particular figures in the incarnation have been well put by a number of contemporary voices. So Bonhoeffer, "Nicht von der Welt zu Gott, sondern von Gott zur Welt geht der Weg Jesus Christi (The way of Christ goes not from this world to God but from God to this world)."[1] So the Southern Baptist educator William Hull, "Flesh for God is not a mask, a disguise, or a subterfuge as the Gnostics supposed. Rather, it is a strategy, a witness, a vehicle for involvement. God's Son wants high visibility in order to be seen and heard and touched by others."[2] And so also, and with great force, the missiologist from Gambia, Lamin Sanneh: "The localization of Christianity is an essential part of the nature of the religion, and . . . without that concrete, historical grounding Christianity becomes nothing but a fragile, elusive abstraction, salt without its saltness. This is the problem which dogs all attempts at defining the core of the gospel as pure dogmatic system without regard to the concrete lives of men and women who call themselves Christian. And it is precisely the historical concreteness of Christianity which makes cross-cultural mutuality possible and meaningful."[3]

Contingent Realities and Christian Politics

If the catalogue of concrete realities displayed in the incarnation is so important for humanity in general, certainly it must be important as well for Christian theorizing about politics. Yet much of the truly important Christian theorizing about politics has tended to be general, abstract, and timeless rather than particular, concrete, and contingent. Harro Höpfl, editor of a helpful anthology of the political writings of Luther and Calvin, notes that although Luther actually propounded several different stances on how Christians should practice politics, each was "general and abstract in form."[4] Each, that is, formulated political advice for Christians from biblical texts, Christian dogmas, supposedly universal human situations, and the dictates of unvarying reason. (In this instance, at least, Luther himself failed to live up to the christological insights I recommended in chapter 3.)

Luther worked out his politics in this relatively abstracted way, however, despite the fact that it is now transparently obvious that the contrasting political conclusions Luther drew at various stages of his career were functions of his own immediate political experience. When the depredations of anti-Protestant rulers were foremost in his mind, Luther's politics moved toward Anabaptist separatism, but when positive support was forthcoming from pro-Protestant princes for reforming the church, Luther's politics accepted a full measure of church-state cooperation.[5] Regarded from the angle of Christ, who was incarnate in the specific circumstances of the rule in Judea of Pontius Pilate, the problem was not that Luther let local circumstances affect his thinking, but that he did not realize how important it was for his own political theorizing to take into account the contingencies of his own situation.

A similar problem obtains for the various changes made by John Calvin in the sections on civil government in book IV, chapter 20 of *The Institutes of the Christian Religion*.[6] In early editions, when the activities of the Catholic king of France against the Protestants and the vacillation of Geneva's councils were uppermost in his mind, the *Institutes* stressed the negative functions of government—the role of the state in restraining evil and allowing space for the church to carry out its own activities. By contrast, in the 1559 edition, when Calvin after prolonged struggle had come to enjoy nearly unanimous support for his church reform from the Geneva councils, he assigned government a much more positive role in supporting not only a truly reformed church but the first table of the Decalogue as well. Significantly, however, as in Luther's case, Calvin consistently reasoned, in 1536 as well as in 1559, from general, abstract, and universal biblical, theological, and philosophical principles, and he did so despite what now seem to be transparent connections between the contingencies of his own circumstances and his conclusions about the nature of Christian political duty. The notion that full, self-conscious attention to shifting political events and circumstances should figure in the formulation of Christian political principles or duties was as absent from Calvin as from Luther.

A similar mode of reasoning prevailed in the creation of neo-Calvinist political thought in the Netherlands during the second half of the nineteenth century. That thinking was principial from beginning to end. It focused on universal, cosmological realities. So it was, for example, that Groen van Prinsterer, in his seminal lectures that gave rise to political neo-Calvinism, could talk of "republicanism" as if it were a universally identical solvent of godly order that always operated in a uniform pattern with a uniform set of baneful consequences. Or as he put the matter from another angle, "Calvinism assuredly never led to any sort of republicanism."[7] Yet from the perspectives of British or American history, it is clear that when Groen thought about "republicanism," he was thinking about a form of political philosophy that had developed in eighteenth-century France and that in nineteenth-century Europe came to be closely linked with various forms of anticlerical secularism. The notion that in other places and in different circumstances—for example, in seventeenth-century Britain or eighteenth-century America—some forms of Calvinism could lead to some forms of republicanism did not fit into the vision of first principles that Groen articulated.

The Politics of Abraham Kuyper

Just about the same comment can be made about the even greater contribution of Abraham Kuyper. At least for Kuyper as politician, Christianity was supremely a life system, a world-and-life view. As James Skillen has summarized the matter, "Kuyper emphasized the need for a comprehensive Christian worldview that would allow for an 'architectonic' or structural critique of the creation's disorder and lead to a multidimensional approach of human service to God and neighbors in all spheres of life."[8] Kuyper himself stated his preference for Calvin over Luther in similar terms by emphasizing the way in which Calvin's theology led naturally to constructing overarching principles for conduct in politics: "Luther as well as Calvin contended for a direct fellowship with God, but Luther took it up from its subjective, anthropological side, and not from its objective, cosmological side as Calvin did. Luther's starting-point was the special-soteriological principle of a justifying faith; while Calvin's, extending far wider, lay in the general cosmological principle of the sovereignty of God."[9]

It seems transparent to an outside observer that specifically Dutch conditions—for example, a tradition of close links between the throne and certain religious advisors—shaped the formulation of Kuyper's political theory. Even more obvious is the way that local conditions channeled the outworking of Kuyper's Christian political theory once he became prime minister of the Netherlands. During his tenure, Kuyper's firm grasp of neo-Calvinist, antirevolutionary political principle certainly shaped his exercise of political power, but so did his decidedly situated actions in cooperating with Roman Catholic political leaders, in urging Britain to moderate its positions during the Boer War, in responding to arguments from the organizers of railroad unions, and in handling the struggle for native rights in Holland's East Asian colonies.[10]

I intend no criticism of what Kuyper taught about the nature of a proper Christian politics, but I do think his political practice would have been even more thoroughly Christian had Kuyper taken more self-consciously into account the contribution of local political conditions to the outworking of his Christian political theory. I add with some trepidation, because of the complexity of the subject, that if Kuyper, as a follower of the Christ incarnate at the time of Pontius Pilate in the period of late-temple Judaism, had acknowledged that his Christian politics were being shaped in part by local conditions in the Netherlands, they would have been less easily misapplied elsewhere. I am thinking specifically of South Africa, where for one subgroup in one Dutch Reformed church Kuyper's political principles became a constituent part of a practical program of apartheid in a local context marked by very different circumstances than prevailed in the Netherlands.[11] Had Kuyper been able to see how some of his Christian principles were directly, and properly, the result of local Dutch conditions, his principles would have been less easily applied where the local context differed so dramatically from his own.

The Particular and the Universal

In sum, attention to a trinitarian doctrine of incarnation, as also to the place of that doctrine in the scheme of the universe, might suggest that Luther, Calvin, Groen, and Kuyper were being too fastidious. Because of the incarnation, in other words, it would have assisted their political reflection to countenance fully their particular circumstances in formulating Christian advice on politics, rather than pretend that they were drawing that advice from Scripture and universal reasoning without the mediation of their own circumstances.

The lesson must surely be that Christian politics, to be truly Christian, must be alert to the circumstances of local cultures as well as to the universal norms of the gospel. Christian political principles from the past are necessary for contemporary Christian politics, but they are not sufficient. None of the great mentors of classical Christian theology did their work in a political situation like ours—not Augustine, not Thomas Aquinas, not Luther, not Calvin, not Abraham Kuyper—that is, where women and the propertyless vote, where popular media have become the forum for promoting political ideas, or where local economies are tied into worldwide economic connections. To think politically as a Christian today, it is necessary to take these realities into account, to heed the multiple meanings of the particulars of human experience, as well as to heed general Christian principles about human nature, the divine economy, and the unchangeable law of God. This counsel for shaping political perspective arises, not from pragmatism, but from a sense of how important the particularities of the incarnation were and are to its meaning. Ideas certainly do have consequences. But as the fact of the appearance of God the Son in human flesh shows so clearly, so do consequences breed ideas.

Conclusion

As an example of how attitudes and perspectives shaped by Christology can affect political reasoning, we can point to the last words of a recent essay by Michael Novak in which he examined the ways in which Christianity shaped the Western political economy. Novak develops his argument in considerable detail and provides readers a full opportunity to assess whether he is interpreting correctly the divinely created realities affecting human nature, the character of freedom, the nature of economic activity, and so forth. But he is also aware that underneath the meaning of Jesus for questions of political economy is the meaning of Jesus for everything. The conclusion to his essay shows how one can give questions in the realm of political economy their due while still remembering the suffering, atoning Savior. I am not necessarily recommending Novak's conclusions about political economy, although they deserve serious attention, but I do think that he has expressed the connections of the realms of christological reality just about as well as they can be expressed: "Better than the philosophers, Jesus Christ is the teacher of many lessons indispensable for the working of the free society. . . . But that alone would be as nothing, of course, if we did not learn from Jesus that we, all of us, participate in His life, and in living with Him, live in, with and through the Father and the Holy Spirit in a glorious community of love. For what would it profit us, if we gained the whole world, and all the free institutions that flourish with it, and lost our own souls?"[1]

Exemplary as Novak's example is, better in this inaugural Kuyper Lecture to end with Abraham Kuyper. In recent years, one of the most bracing encouragements to think and act like Christians in the political sphere has been to hear contemporary neo-Calvinists like Richard Mouw, James Skillen, or Nicholas Wolterstorff quote the spine-tingling tocsin that Kuyper first declaimed 115 years ago at the opening of the Free University of Amsterdam. "There is not an inch," he roared, "not an inch in the entire domain of our human life of which Christ, who is sovereign of all, does not proclaim 'Mine.'"[2]

Politically considered, no truer words could ever be spoken. They convey the dramatic picture of Christ transfigured in glory, hand outstretched, finger extended in commanding power, standing over the halls of Congress, the White House, the United Nations, the state legislature, the local school board, the tax assessor's office, and the weary citizen sitting at home and reading the front page of the local newspaper, and declaring with full yet winsome authority, "This too is mine!" Yet it may be that this picture is not quite complete, for the footprints of the Jesus who points to every one of our political institutions, to every one of our political practices, to every one of our political theories, and claims each one as his very own, are footprints spattered with blood. And the hand that points is marked with a wound. Our politics will be a Christian politics if we follow the commanding Christ as he takes possession of the world, but it will be a fully Christian politics only if we remember the road to Calvary that the Lord Jesus took to win his place of command, and never forget that the robes of the saints shine white only because they are washed in the blood of the Lamb.

Cross, Crown, and Kuyper's Legacy

Response by James D. Bratt

Mark Noll has launched the Kuyper Lecture series with grace. I mean that word theologically. Few voices, if any, can match his at conveying sharp critique in a pastoral tone, at combining spiritual insight and historical knowledge, at blending passion for the church with dispassionate scrutiny of self. Noll shows some aesthetic grace as well, as when he judges some Christian political parties to have been "half right, and therefore doubly dangerous"; in reminding us that "the kingdom that must be entered as a child offers full and satisfying work for adults"; in his disarming, unsettling opening: "I want to explore the difference it might make if Christian politics featured Christ." His paper does not claim to be the last word on its subject; it is rather the opening word of a conversation that *does* need to be reopened. For

James D. Bratt (Ph.D., Yale University) is professor of history at Calvin College where he teaches American religious history. He is the author of *Dutch Calvinism in Modern America* (Grand Rapids: Eerdmans, 1984) and *Gathered at the River: Grand Rapids, Michigan and Its People of Faith* (Grand Rapids: Eerdmans, 1993). He is currently working on an anthology of the political writings of Abraham Kuyper.

the care and cogency with which he has accomplished this, we should be grateful.

His topic is quite appropriate to an inaugural Kuyper Lecture, for cross as well as crown loomed large in the thought of the person for whom this series is named. Abraham Kuyper's biographer says that the most moving document he has come across in his years of research on the man is a letter Kuyper wrote to his daughter in the Dutch East Indies in 1903. Facing the railroad strike that would cripple his political career, the prime minister and father wrote: "My calling is high, my task is glorious. Above my bed hangs a crucifix, and when I look up there it is as if the Lord is asking me each night: 'What is your struggle next to my bitter cup?' His service is so exalting and glorious."[1]

Kuyper's bed, crowned with the cross: The image is deeply personal. The issue for him was also theological, and Kuyper did his part to carry on the passion of Reformed dogmatics for the order of salvation; but where is the cross in Kuyper's politics? I must say, I don't know. This is partly because I have not looked for it—evidence enough, perhaps, of the need to reopen the matter—and partly because the Kuyper scholars whom I have read have not said much about it either. My supposition, based on considerable study of the Dutch Reformed tradition on both sides of the Atlantic, is this: For Kuyper and the political tradition he bred, the cross is private or personal, lifted up in the inner chamber of one's salvation story but not lifted up in the public square. There Kuyperians have followed the order of creation, not of redemption. Kuyper made this clear at a high-water mark in his career, on the occasion of his silver jubilee as newspaper editor, when he delivered himself of the following *apologia pro vita sua:* "One desire rules my life, one urge drives soul and will: . . . to re-establish . . . in church and home, in state and school . . . those divine ordinances to which Word and Creation attest . . . so that the nation bows its knee to God once again."[2] Creation ordinances and national obedience are the dominant themes here, not redemption, grace, and liberation. The latter themes certainly are present in Kuyper's thought, but at this signal moment, he left them hidden.

Dangers of a Cross-Centered Politics

Noll thinks such a cross-crown divide presents a problem, and I agree. It also has its virtues, however, and as we examine Noll's remedy for the problem, we need to think about how to preserve these. Put negatively, in pushing the conversation forward we need to take account of how we are going to negotiate the dangers *of* and the dangers *to* bringing the cross, the order of redemption, back into the public square.

The dangers of such a reintroduction are apparent in what remains our most noxious image of political cross-bearing, namely, the shields and flags of the medieval Crusaders. Less egregiously but closer to our own situation, cross-raising might well be taken to mean an eclipse of confessional pluralism in public life. Yet Kuyper's noblest contribution to Dutch history, and to his North American legacy, was precisely his striking down of confessional imperialism by declaring that the Netherlands was no longer simply a Christian nation and that Christians should learn to live, even be glad, in that. Kuyper turned to the order of creation because he thought all citizens had that in common and could make a politically workable, though not identical, reference to it. The world's three great monotheisms share the First Person of the Trinity, and even Enlightenment-derived natural law theory can recognize that Person as analogue, but symbols associated with the Second Person are tradition specific. Since common life requires common ground, Kuyper put politics under common, not special, grace.

The other danger lies in the prospect that cross-bearing might make our politics ineffectual. Here I am recalling an old controversy in Dutch-American circles that began with the arrival of Kuyperian enthusiasts in the quarter century before World War I. Their opponents derided their proposal for confessional politics as "unrealistic," meaning that however appropriate a Christian political party might be in the Netherlands, it was wholly out of place in the United States since American politics was either properly secular or thoroughly irredeemable or already Christian under the aegis of the Republican Party. (Some critics managed to make all three suggestions in a row.)[3] Now Noll is not proposing a Christian political party but a Christian political ethic, an attitude or approach of humility and self-criticism, one that defends the other's—and especially the poor's—rights first. Still, one must ask: Is anything less likely to succeed at this juncture in American history? Or lest we be too present-minded, at any juncture? Let us recall that Timothy Dwight, as close an analogue to Kuyper as American Calvinism might have to offer, did not hesitate in the presidential election of 1800 to raise the most fearful specters against Thomas Jefferson for purposes of defending what he treasured as a holy way of life, the remnant of his Puritan ancestors' privilege.

From the gentlemanly Dwight's time onward, mobilization in American politics, and particularly in popular Christian politics, has depended on a rhetoric of sensationalism, conspiracy mongering, and forthright appeals to group power or national pride. Running through the political history, and especially the Christian political history, of this country is not a posture of cross-bearing, nor even one of recovering creational foundations, but a theology that one of Kuyper's Dutch-American disciples in 1918 characterized as *chiliastische droomerijen*, millenarian fantasies.[4] Here is "crown theology" indeed: the iron rod of apocalyptic revenge with which one brains the enemy of the moment in the name of Jesus the Judge. My question then is twofold: Has not a Kuyperian creation theology at least played out better than this? And given the persistence for over two hundred years of the rhetorical and theological devices I have named, where and how in the American world will a humble politics of the cross be mounted? If the reply be that Christians are called to faithfulness not success, the answer remains the same today as it was in Dutch America a century ago: Maybe a Christian need not be successful, but a Christian politician who is not successful will not long be a politician.

Surely that conclusion by itself is the counsel of despair. It begs the question of what constitutes success, a question that needs to be answered from theology, political theory, and a close reading of history attentive to the mighty consequences of small beginnings. Complaints about "impractical idealism" can also spell, as our old Dutch Americans showed, acquiescence in either conceptual or strategic error or in a species of cultural idolatry. Whatever their shortcomings or misapplications, Kuyper's stand on principle and his insistence that Christianity be consistent and thoroughgoing ought to inspire believers everywhere to put off such acquiescence and consider again what the faithful are called to do. Noll's analysis, combining as it does theology, theory, and historical scrutiny, sheds new light on that task.

What does Noll's analysis illuminate? It illuminates first of all an inconsistency in Kuyper's own attempt to be consistent. Kuyperians have been quick to spy out dualism, particularly a strict separation of religion and politics. Kuyper's own rhetoric, however, bespoke all sorts of dualities: inner-outer, kernel-husk, common-particular, principle-practice, high-low. The cross-crown–private-public analogy I have already touched on points to a dualist premise beneath Kuyper's whole project, namely, the Victorian divide of gender roles that he inherited and that he did his best to pass on to the future.

The qualities that Kuyper and his contemporaries sought in the conversion experience under the cross were understood as "female": anguish, tears, quiet patience, self-subjugation, and final calm. Men might (Dutch Calvinist men *had to*) run this gauntlet in the inner chamber of their souls, but then they faced a problem in taking the cross public. Aptly, Kuyper's moving words about the crucifix over his bed came in a letter to his daughter, a nobly female missionary nurse in the colonies. His own conversion was triggered and mentored by women: the English novelist Charlotte Yonge, whose *Heir of Redclyffe* moved Kuyper, by his own account, through precisely the series of cross-qualities listed above; and Pietje Baltus, a village spinster at his first parish, whose stubborn intercessions opened his eyes to the living legacy of Calvin.[5] Looking back at Kuyper under Noll's insistence that we reassess cross and crown thus brings us to a renewed confrontation with the meanings of masculine and feminine for soul and society, for political thought and practice.

Noll's refraction of political theology through the incarnation, on the other hand, yields less clarity on two counts. First, it is not evident from his account why the incarnation associates principally with the cross. Why does incarnation spell Calvary instead of, say, Bethlehem? After all, Christ became incarnate by birth, not by death; and if the death is the point of the story, then it seems to this theological amateur that something more than incarnation is needed to tell the story well. Second, for all the theological nuance the incarnation affords us, for all the valorizing of our humanity and history that it mandates, the politics that follows out of that doctrine tends to bear more conservative consequences than Noll would likely be comfortable with. Whether this correlation is systemically necessary I will leave to others better qualified to say, but a quick scan of the historical record is not reassuring. Lutheran and Orthodox communities, to take two traditions more emphatic on the incarnation than are the Reformed, are not renowned for defying absolute rule, for criticizing privilege masquerading as tradition, or for questioning authority gone authoritarian.

To cut closer to home, Latter-Day Saints do not shirk at a physical, contextualized Christ but rather double his incarnations and locate one in America, a move with political normative implications that are troubling indeed. If the political sacralizations of the New Christian Right are disturbing, what about a body that does not even need to cross a bridge from church to nation but places the former in the heart of the latter? On the other hand, keeping the incarnation within the bounds of apostolic orthodoxy might, though not always, avoid these rocks only to run onto those of political quietism. Here an American example that should be dear to Reformed hearts might prove instructive.

John Williamson Nevin (1803–86) did more than anyone else to recover for American Protestantism the Reformation's emphasis on the church, John Calvin's teaching on the sacraments, the patristic roots of both, and a sense of the church's unity across time and space. All these grew precisely out of his robust view of the incarnation, but what happened to Nevin politically? Heir to a stalwart antislavery tradition (his father debated college classmate Roger Taney, and Nevin himself defended Theodore Weld's protest at Lane Seminary), his "churchly" conversion coincided with his move to Mercersberg Seminary near Lancaster, Pennsylvania. There, hard by the Mason-Dixon line, he said nothing about slavery for the twenty years (1840–60) when that issue defined American politics, and as the Civil War ground on while Nevin was professor of history at Franklin and Marshall College, he had almost nothing public to say about the momentous history happening literally in his own backyard.[6]

The moral of these stories is that a renewed emphasis on the incarnation might do wonderful things for American Protestants, especially the evangelicals among them. It might also do good things for Christian political reflection and action. But then again, it might not. It all depends on the people doing the acting and reflecting, on how the rest of the theological constellation figures with the incarnational star, and we might say, on doing good history as well as good theology and political philosophy. This methodological point, I believe, is crucial. To see how and why that is so, we need to retrace the circuit of Kuyperian theoretical practice for a moment and see how Noll's approach may support, supplement, or challenge it.

Benefits of a Cross-Centered Politics

Kuyper always insisted that he started from principle—in theology, in political philosophy, in the charter of his university, in the editorials in his daily newspaper. Not surprisingly, this habit generated a mighty legacy of philosophers and systematic theologians. It was a power, if not *the* power, that launched the perspectival approach that is riding high in North American Christian academia. It gave him confidence to withstand the academic orthodoxies of his time, which covered naturalism and positivism in the cloak of objectivity. It taught his followers to think systematically, to treat issues holistically, to rise above theology-by-the week and politics-of-gut-instinct. It has produced, among many other institutions, the Center for Public Justice, which sponsors this series. I am not patronizing the patron, however, in reciting this litany of praise. Kuyper's architectonic thinking is a powerful and worthy tool that should not and cannot be casually discarded.

It should not be casually used or turned into a bludgeon, however. Something of that criticism lies behind Noll's protest against the abstraction and universalizing pretense of some of Kuyper's thinking. The point is well taken; in fact, examples of the fault can be multiplied far beyond those Noll adduces. Kuyper celebrated the United States's victory in the Spanish-American War—until the McKinley administration refused to shift its support from the British to the Boers in South Africa; then he accused America of principial error. Likewise with British foreign policy shifts from 1880 to 1900—these could not be understood as geopolitical but had to be religiously retrograde in motivation. Kuyper read the United States as New England, New England as simply Puritan, the Glorious Revolution as Cromwellian, Nietzscheans and positivists as identically pantheistic, the French Revolution as but philosophy on wheels, Roman Catholicism here as Christian, there as antichrist. He too was often "half right, and therefore doubly . . ."—I would not say "dangerous," for he exercised little legal power on these occasions; "misleading" might serve better. Very often a propagandist, he resorted to careless, all-too-convenient, and yes, abstract philosophizing.

Would the correction Noll suggests take care of the problem? Was Kuyper, and implicitly, Kuyperians of all ages with him, guilty of too apodictic an application of abstract principles, of too little sensitivity to local circumstances? Or was the opposite the case—that he was not consistent enough, that he trimmed and dodged toward a foreordained policy goal and pushed principle around until it fit? The South African example Noll raises is an apt case in point. Far better, it would seem, for Kuyper—and Kuyperians—to have held fast to the principle he enunciated with respect to northern Europe and the United States, that racial mixing produces finer nations than does homogeneity; to have stuck to the principle of small government and so to have resisted the turn to a gargantuan state-security apparatus; to have made good on his claim that Calvinism in principle was committed to, and in historical fact was the guarantor of, constitutional liberties rather than to have elaborated the arbitrary oppressions of apartheid. Kuyper's positive legacy in North America, it seems to me, stems precisely from his followers' insistence on measuring national and civil religious claims against the ultimate claims of a universal church, against Christian political principles that derived precisely from another source than North American local conditions.

Am I suggesting that Christian politics be more universalized, or more localized? More contextually nuanced, or more philosophically consistent? The answer is yes—both, together, all the time. It is the separation of the two— Kuyper's claim to be thinking from the heavens, ignoring his two-step on the ground; his American opponents' "practicality," blind to their governing premises—that is the cause of a lot of our problems, and it is only their intermeshing that can render a solution. This reiteration of the obvious is necessary because it entails some less obvious methodological and disciplinary implications. It means that we cannot concoct a perfect, or even decent, political theory and only then proceed to practice. It means we should stop pretending that we consult Scripture or principled norms and only then make a statement about this or that hot issue, when we have in fact decided the matter instinctively and then rooted about for sufficient biblical legitimation. It means that "consequences breed ideas," so that Christian political thinkers need to be not only philosophers and ethicists but historians as well.

The Center for Public Justice has distinguished itself in fact by this very sensitivity. None of the criticism I have just voiced is meant to fault its work. But the tradition behind CPJ and the habits of many on the Christian Right and the Christian Left today too often pretend that this is the way they work. They have thus deluded others; worse yet, Reinhold Niebuhr would say, they have deluded themselves. In 1898 Kuyper ended his Princeton lecture on "Calvinism and Science" with the plea that confessional honesty, the forthright declaration of one's ruling principles, might produce real progress in scholarship.[7] A hundred years later, we need to say that honesty about how our real-world affinities help shape our professed principles is necessary for progress in the Christian schools of politics.

What is to prevent our hastening under this new candor to rubber-stamp our meanest interest with pragmatic sanction? Noll would press "the particularities of the incarnation" as a theological restraint. His own conduct in this paper is a compelling practical model. He does not try to hide where he stands on the American political spectrum. His discomfort with the confidences and posturing of the Christian Right quite evidently informs his call for a greater sense of humility, paradox, and grace. He does not set out to define a "Reformed view" of politics; of such the Kuyperian tradition already has enough. He would add, rather, some "seasoning" from our recollection of Christ's suffering to our mental picture of Christ's triumphant rule. He would, in his favorite image, add Lutheran leaven to a Calvinist lump. In that, he exemplifies the multidisciplinary, interactive thinking that is needed to weave principle, example, custom, and theology together into an understanding of how the world works and of how we are to judge its workings.

Conclusion

No doubt Noll's approach raises methodological problems. Practitioners from a given domain will doubtless find fault with his incompleteness on their particular turf. The theologian will wonder, given all of his attention to the First and Second Persons, where the Third Person of the Trinity fits into the picture. The historian will say that the whole story at any one point is much more complex than he implies. The consistently Reformed or Lutheran or Orthodox devotee will protest the syncretism at play here. All this is good—good because interweavers such as Noll need to be challenged by specialists who can pose unasked questions and spy out unforeseen implications; and good also because such protests are sure tokens that the ice jams of conventional discourse are being sliced open, allowing the waters to flow freely again.

Besides, unbeknownst to most, Noll's example calls up the subtextual mode of Kuyper's own operations. That much is clear from the disclosure that Kuyper originally titled his first lecture at Princeton, the urtext of the principled worldview approach, not "Calvinism a Life-System," as it has come down in published form, but "Calvinism in History."[8] The argument in this lecture, and not this one alone, proceeds indeed quite as much by historical commentary as by theoretical articulation.

Kuyper started out professionally as a church historian, studied the seventeenth century closely, cultivated a baroque style, and postulated all reality as development from first principles. He galvanized his followers by telling them a metastory, so deftly weaving their parochial situation into a grand global narrative of divine mandate and human struggle as to propel them into writing the next chapter. True, some of the principal actors in this story were philosophical, and the tale could best be comprehended by those adept in theory. Ideas mattered for Kuyper, however, when they had legs and strode into the thick stream of human life. It is also true that Kuyper's storytelling could push beyond the assertive into the aggressive, but that was a fault of substance, not mode. Noll weaves a more cautionary tale with a view to warning an overconfident Right. So whom should we follow, Noll or Kuyper? Both, neither, maybe each by half, depending on the situation. No theory or theology arrayed just so will relieve our need for judgment. Both need to be built upon and looped back into wisdom, discerning the moment and the movement of the times.

The Kuyper Lecture series thus begins on an auspicious note, modeling and inviting a nuanced dialogue. The conversation it opens should aim to cultivate a sensitivity and sensibility more than a philosophy. It should leave behind the hope of getting all possible cases into a box and tying it up in a bow. For Kuyperians that prospect is difficult to entertain—maybe for intellectuals and would-be political masters too. If none of the other challenges in Noll's essay has theological warrant, this one surely does.

To accept a measure of human uncertainty is to confess that we are not God. To go forward without everything having been theoretically determined in advance requires that we as Christians trust each other to be genuinely committed to working out our faith in practice, and our practice in faith, and that we rely on each other to teach and learn such faithfulness as we go along. In other words, it requires us to be the church. Maybe this is the mediating role for that institution that Kuyperians and others who champion mediating social structures need most to discover for themselves: That as an ecumenical body, joined over time and space and multifarious specializations, the church contains the experience and the communion needed to cross over between system and subtlety, the wisdom and forgiveness that can embolden people to take risks, withstand fads, and learn from error. Such a mediation is worthy of the body that calls itself, and is called to be, the living presence of the one who died on the cross so as to win for us a crown.

Public Theology
and Christological Politics

Response by Max L. Stackhouse

When a former Presbyterian from Colorado and a former
Catholic from Cuba, both converts to the tradition stemming
from Kuyper, invite a former Methodist from Indiana who
was converted to the ecumenical tradition through reading
Lutherans and Puritans, to respond to an evangelical from
Canada now teaching at Wheaton who celebrates the insights of Luther in an address to several hundred Dutch
scholars and church leaders at Calvin College, I know that I
am at some sort of reunion of an extended family. I am de-
lighted to join those whom I immediately recognize as
relatives.

In regard to Cousin Mark Noll, I have to begin by noting
that his contributions to evangelical scholarship and challenges to evangelical scholars are rarely matched, and his

Max L. Stackhouse (Ph.D., Harvard University) is Stephen Colwell Professor of
Christian ethics at Princeton Theological Seminary, where he moved after a distinguished teaching career at Andover Newton Theological School. He has authored
scores of articles and several books, including *Creeds, Society and Human Rights*
(Grand Rapids: Eerdmans, 1984), *Public Theology and Political Economy* (Grand
Rapids: Eerdmans, 1987), and *Christian Ethics and Economic Life* (Nashville: Abingdon Press, 1995).

combination of irenic spirit and inspired energy is widely appreciated. The whole family can be proud that he is one of us. Surely he has an important question to put to us: He wants to know what difference Christology makes in politics, what "difference it could make for Christians to concentrate on the person and work of Christ when they think about politics or when they engage in political activity."

Noll believes that politics must be seen in light of the incarnation and the cross, and while he shows great sympathy for the resurgence of Christian influence in public life, he is hesitant about the triumphalism visible in some advocates of a crusading Christianity. He makes a number of observations about particular historical movements, all seen through the lens captured by the logo of his school, "For Christ and His Kingdom." In this connection, he tends to identify Calvinism with "kingly rule," and to that he wants to add the leaven of Lutheran "cross-centeredness." The more obvious reason for his inquiry is the rise of the Christian Coalition, which is making political waves in ways few anticipated; the less obvious one is his reservation about the magisterial impulses of many in the Reformed tradition.

The Resurgence of Religion in Public Life

What Noll has noted, however, may not be solely a Christian phenomenon. It seems to me to be quite clear that Islam, Hinduism, and Buddhism, not to mention the so-called New Age religions, which are mostly old paganisms revived, are also in resurgence and again seeking political influence.[1] What is going on, I think, are three things at once.

First, the nation-state is declining in importance precisely because a new global society is rising in our very midst. This global society is putting constraints on what the nation-state can accomplish on its own, even as it puts special pressures on the United States to assume the role of world leader.

Second, many now believe that important issues of public life require greater local attention and more nuance treatment than huge national bureaucracies can efficiently provide. It simply does not seem possible that federal policy alone can deal with many of the problems that are eroding our civil society—the divorce rate, the morals of the generation, the sense of a loss of community, or personal feelings of failure. More fell with the fall of the Berlin Wall than the central-command economies of Eastern Europe and the mercantilist one-party states; the vision of an all-encompassing political order that could guide the whole of life also fell. We now face altered roles in family life; new areas of science, education, and the professions; massive influences of technology, communication, and media; the exploding impact of corporations; and half a dozen lesser forces, all of which are at once more local and more far-reaching than any government.[2]

Third, and most important, there is a rising awareness that a foundation for civilization—locally, nationally, or globally—cannot be based either on what the Enlightenment called "human rationality" or on what the romantics celebrated as "human creativity." Both of these attempted to locate the supernatural entirely within the processes and dynamics of human nature.[3] While we recognize that every society requires a responsible government, and while we continue to appreciate the sciences and arts that claim rootage in some forms of humanism, the common life cannot stand on these bases alone. These areas are themselves not self-sufficient; they require religion. The key question then is what kind of religion comes to predominate in public life. Some of us hold that Christian faith, with its deep sense of common grace and general revelation, can best nurture the deep social architecture that makes the arts and sciences as well as government more viable, open, and nonoppressive.

The other two changes already mentioned, however, bring us immediately into the presence of multiple religious traditions, each experiencing neopopulist self-rediscovery and ready to engage in highly assertive policies. The presence of multiple religions could, of course, evoke a practical pluralism, but more often it leads to intense conflict, for it is in the nature of each of the great religious traditions that each seeks to guide the whole of the civilization. In multicultural contexts, though, every religious claim is more difficult to sustain. Faiths confront not only counterfaiths but also secular ideologies purporting not to be faiths. Not a few presume that they have a responsibility to advance their faith by political power and feel driven to prove the truth of that faith by making it dominate all of life. A subtlety about the way in which faith relates to power is thus required from the start.

It is with these issues in mind that I turn to the three major questions raised in Noll's essay: (1) Would not a focus on the person and work of Christ reduce the tendency toward the aggressiveness he sees in the Reformed focus on the kingdom of God? (2) Should not politics mean a kind of governmental policy that is focused on the concrete and that includes local tradition and practice? (3) Would it not be better if our view of politics was filtered through the attitudes that the incarnate and crucified Christ engenders in us? Noll contends that if we move in the direction he suggests, we will approach political life in a way that is more open to contingencies than much of triumphal Christian politics has been in the past and threatens to become again. I will raise questions about each of these three areas, with greatest focus on the first.

Christology and the Trinity

Noll begins with the person and work of Christ within the context of the Trinity, because it is, he says, "inescapably the starting point for all Christian reflection, including Christian reflection on politics." In taking this point of departure, he differs with those in the Catholic and Reformational traditions who start from a creational point of view—natural law, orders of creation, general revelation—and, in view of the fall, seek an eschatological restoration, fulfillment, and transformation of the world in accordance with God's original law and ultimate purpose. The process of bringing that vision to fulfillment is often identified with the presence of the kingdom within history.[4] Noll suspects that this starting point involves an effort to see things from God's point of view and thus is in danger of forgetting that we are not God and have to see things from the standpoint of fallen sinners saved only by the grace of God whom we know in Christ.

It is surely the case that Christians call themselves Christians because they start their reflection in Christ: The person and work of Christ is decisive for our lives. It may also be, however, that we can turn to Christ because God created the world good and preserves it by his providential grace, even in its fallen condition. It may be true as well that we, as the early Christians recognized, have to move to a larger frame of reference when we begin to address public issues beyond the church. It is not by accident that the longest and deepest debates in Christianity have been over the doctrine of the Trinity, in which Christ is located within a larger systematic and narrative framework as one person among the Three in One.[5] In other words, Christ may well be the center of how we come to know God in our personal lives, but Christ may not be the whole of everything that God is and does in relationship to the world, especially the political world.[6]

We can see this when we think about other areas of life. To hold that Christ is Lord does not tell us all that Christians can and must do to be faithful in economic life, even though the term *Lord (kurios, dominus, seigneur, Herr, heer)* is drawn from economic affairs. Or we may hold that Christ is the great Rabbi, the religiously authoritative Teacher, as his disciples said, but that belief does not determine the whole of an academic curriculum, even in a Christian college. Similarly, if we are to take Christ as our guide in political matters, it is likely that we have to have a larger framework in which to locate and properly identify the center point. The issue then is whether the context does not itself demand a theological comprehension that allows us to rightly identify the person and work of Christ.

When we speak of the person of Christ, we are immediately drawn into a discussion of his two natures as fully human and fully divine. The very particular, highly contextual, and historically conditioned Jesus of Nazareth is confessed also to be the totally universal, transcontextual, and eternal God. When we personally take this Jesus as our Lord and Savior, we affirm that the universal, transcontextual, and eternal is present in particular, contextual, and temporal realities, and that the ordinary difference between these realms is somehow overcome. This affirmation means, as Noll recognizes, the necessity of taking particular, concrete, historical factors seriously. Christ is not only incarnate, however, he is also resurrected and ascended. I shall have more to say later about resurrection; for now, let me simply point out that in American Protestant piety, both evangelical and ecumenical, Ascension Day is hardly noted. Now, it is not at all clear that a more intense focus on it in the church calendar would completely alter our perspective on matters, but it seems to this observer that one of the great gifts of the evangelical traditions in this country is the accent on the transcontingent, even transhistorical, reality of Christ. This accent is at least a tacit recognition that in the ascension some particulars are raised to a new level of universal and eternal triumph over the messy pluralism and historical contingency of the world.

The uniqueness of the person of Christ also means that not all traditions and practices in family life, national identity, custom, and culture are equally to be sanctified, as Noll's quote from Andrew Walls suggests should be the case. In Walls's view, what is advocated seems to be a general embrace of, even the celebration of, a vast array of particulars, a view fully in accord with the current antistructuralism of the postmodernists. What is important about the particulars from a christological point of view, however, is that some particulars bear the marks of the universal more clearly than others. This has direct political implications, for whether Noll is correct or not, he will have to define the universal as clearly as he has embraced the notion of christological particularity. How else is he to defend the claim that Canada tends to combine the particular and the universal in ways that more closely approximate the incarnation than does the United States, or that political justice in the new South Africa "will incorporate aspects of traditional tribal hierarchicalism"?

We may ask further whether the focus on the person of Christ may not need to be supplemented by a focus on the work of Christ. Paul writes of the "already–not yet" character of the work of Christ, but today we face a number of opinions to the effect that everything is already accomplished, and that what we have, therefore, is only a mopping-up operation—one, some say, that must be accomplished by us in Christ's name without violence or coercion or war or imperial power. The implicit pacifism of this view has made for some odd alliances with the Anabaptist traditions among American evangelicals. Noll seems to share this view when he suggests that if we perceive the political world through the perspective of Christ, we will reduce the role of power in politics.

The notion of the *simul*—that we are, until the kingdom comes, simultaneously justified and sinners—which Noll takes from the Lutherans, may be more correct on this point, however, for it requires a realism about political power that all could learn better if Lutherans did not keep telling us that it is their doctrine alone. It also provides a better way to understand the inevitable necessity of engagement with coercive power than the "two kingdoms" idea of those who have pushed the law-gospel distinction into a separation of faith from politics or tied their views to an Anabaptist opposition to culture.[7] In short, the *simul* may allow us to see both the basic distinction as well as the necessary connection between Christ and Caesar.

To raise such matters is to point to larger issues, including the question of the relation of Christology to the doctrine of the Trinity as it bears on issues of politics, and the question of how American evangelicals should relate to the Orthodox, Catholic, and ecumenical traditions. The core of the doctrine of the Trinity is that God is best understood, in God's own inner life and in relation to the world, as a society of persons who combine the narrative of creation, fall, and redemption with a structured pattern of an eternal tri-unity that defies monolithic, dualistic, and polytheistic views of both the divine and human reality.

Noll is clear that he wants to see Christ in the context of the Trinity, but neither the other Persons of the Trinity nor the concept of a dynamic structure seen as a whole play an overt role in his thinking. To be sure, he has a place for the notion of God the Creator and Lawgiver, but he is suspicious of it since it tends, in his view, to lead to a theocracy that loses sight of the cross. When this view becomes political, he says, it tends toward a Christian politics that features "themes of righteousness, holiness, and commandment-keeping more closely associated with doctrines of a restored creation" rather than those of humility and repentance.

Noll does have a point, and we each could give illustrations of theocratic advocacy that loses sight of the tenderness, pain, and forgiveness of the cross, but so far this is simply an either-or debate. One of the key aspects of the doctrine of the Trinity, however, is the implication that there are never simply two options. There is always a third possibility that needs to be taken into account, and it is only when all three are involved that we begin to grasp the ever-renewing dynamism and the constant logic of the whole. Without both Christ and the Holy Spirit and all they bring in terms of novelty, communion, and sanctification, as Kuyper knew and some of his disciples forgot, a theocratic monotheism of the First Person can ignore the prophetic, transformative dimension of eschatology and turn restorationist, with all that this entails in terms of the reactive drive toward the *status quo ante.*

A monotheism of the Second Person, on the other hand, as H. Richard Niebuhr accused Karl Barth of perpetrating on our age, and as some evangelicals seem to embrace, turns everything into a concreteness of the personal or particular. Here there is little care either for the normative orders of law embedded in the very fabric of creation and the insights of the prophets who call society to justice under the enduring terms of God's covenant, or for the humanity-wide relevance of the catholic and ecumenical church—all of which the creed treats under the Holy Spirit. To be sure, the temptation to a monotheism of the Third Person that we find in Pentecostalism has its own problems, but that is not in debate at the moment. It could well be, however, that this monotheism will be the future of an evangelicalism that does not reach toward systemic thinking and teaching.

The Trinity disallows above all the tendency to make any one of its members the fullness of the whole, a matter critical as we relate theology to politics. Unless the doctrines of creation and of the Holy Spirit are accented, we can easily lose the sense that humanity lives under a reliable law of universal justice as well as a dynamic openness to religious, intellectual, and spiritual movements outside the specific community of Christ. We would then be tempted to identify the nation with the church, and to offer a full place of citizenship only to those who have a personal experience of Christ, which is precisely what a number of Jewish leaders think the Christian Coalition and the evangelical resurgence today portends. In contrast, the Trinity, as spelled out in its political implications, makes the world safe for pluralism in a way that few, and perhaps no other, views of God do.

All this is to suggest that while the Trinity reserves a very high place for each person of the Godhead, it demands that each be treated within a social view of the nature and character of God. Reality in its ultimate normative character indeed is viewed as the vibrant and mutually reinforcing pluralism of interacting persons that cannot be reduced to one of its parts. This reality is a highly abstract and systemic view, but that is just the point. It simply is not clear that the evangelical accent on personal piety, as indispensable as this is, is adequate to the task of serious engagement with the cosmopolitan world of politics—or science or law or technology. Armed with the doctrine of the Trinity, however, the church defied the attempt of Constantine and his theological advocates to decide the future of civilization.[8] The Trinity demanded that a context be established wherein the church could flourish and, in obedience to Christ, seek the victory of the Holy Spirit over the spirits of the world in the secrets of the human heart and the interactions of communities—the family and the economy, academia and the arts—while recognizing the role of political authority to protect, on the basis of a cosmopolitan law and by the proper use of force against destructive evil, the social space in which the battles for the heart and mind of humanity could be conducted.[9]

The church understood itself as the body of Christ to be the center or decisive core of civil society. It was on that basis that it sought to establish God's reign in every sector of civilization while limiting, by its own existence, the sphere of political power. The church's life depended on theological affirmations for which political orders, even imperial ones, were not competent. It did not deny, however, the distinctive role that politics had to play; indeed it gradually became clear after the Reformation that every believer is also a citizen and has the duty to participate in the exercise of political authority. While it is true that many believers could not tell the difference between Constantine's dreaming vision of the cross (*in hoc signo vinces,* "conquer under this sign") and the rational architectonic grasp of the ultimate interplay of order and dynamism that the church articulated for the whole, the two together allowed the faithful to seek the reality of *Christus victor* in the hearts and souls of the people, and to develop, in a long and complicated historical drama, an open, pluralistic, democratic polity as a manifestation of the life of faith.

We must, as Noll recognizes, be extremely careful here, for if we get the priorities backward, as did Pope Urban II only a few centuries after Constantine, we are tempted to invite the political warriors of the day to take the sign of the cross on them.[10] Some say, in fact, that the idea of the crusade was only ended when Napoleon defeated Malta in 1798, although others contend that it did not die at all and is now resplendent in the resurgence of piety seeking to seize political power. When we call for the taking on of the cross in addressing political matters, it is thus vitally important that we recognize the ambiguities in Christian history when this has been attempted.

One might note here, as Noll does, that some Reformation authors, such as Calvin, Ursinus, Bullinger, and many Puritans, attempted to work more directly with the centrality of Christ. They very quickly turned, however, to matters of covenant and anthropology (the "old" and "new" Adam),[11] and to the offices of Christ, which as it turns out are public, theological, and rather obviously trinitarian in structure. Every society of persons requires a sphere in which prophetic, priestly, and political responsibilities can be exercised without undue interference from the others, if each is to flourish. Both the Kuyperian tradition and much contemporary scholarship on the relationship of biblical themes to political themes understand this fact.[12] In looking for Christian approaches to politics, therefore, the evangelical wing of the Protestant and ecumenical families must press for a wider consideration of the wisdom of the tradition that stands between the Scriptures and present movements. This tradition argues for the necessary priority of Trinity to Christology, and for the importance of diversified understandings of covenant and of office, which the Anabaptists, many evangelicals, and a great number of ecumenical Christians have ignored.[13]

Politics in the Concrete

The relevance of the issues raised above quickly becomes clear when we turn our attention to politics, for a social theory of God implies a social theory of politics. When Christianity established the church as the center of civil society, commending the individual to become conformed to Christ and the empire to the Trinity, the political order was no longer seen as the comprehending order of governance. It was seen instead under an ultimately unified but pluriform God as one among a number of necessary, functional, useful, institutional sectors of the common life called into being with a specific vocation from God. Each was to be subjected to the influence both of personal discipline, through those who were true to the God whom they knew through Jesus Christ, and of the laws and procedures proper to its own vocation within a complex web of societal clusters.

There have been many efforts to name the various institutional areas of society—estates, orders, spheres, mandates—to identify exactly how many there are and to specify how they ought to be related. These remain matters of ongoing debate, but all recognize that something is prior to the political order.[14] Liberationists and libertarians, for example, know that something is prior to politics, although one group speaks of class relations based on the organization of the means of production, and the other speaks of social contracts based on the will of individuals. Conservatives and nationalists also know that something is prior to politics, although conservatives might point to tradition, and nationalists to the spirit of the people. All agree, however, with the Christian claim that something other than politics makes civil society, and that politics can only be viable when it recognizes this and confines itself to its proper role.

Where Christians differ from these various schools of thought is in the belief that the decisive "something" is more radical than class, contract, inherited tradition, or national spirit. There is a community of identity that is more profound than all or any of these—the church, the body of Christ, which is partly visible and partly invisible. It is partly invisible because the power of these other forces ever influences our lives and mixes with the identity we have. It becomes partly visible where, by the power of the Spirit, the Word is rightly preached and the sacraments rightly performed so that persons are empowered to engage and shape the several arenas of the common life. Christ thus faces not only politics but all the powers of society—of Techne and of Mammon, of the Muses and of Eros, since these too bear the marks of their origin in the Creator even when they go awry.

The body of Christ and its members face these powers in their own dens and seek to prevent them from seizing politics and turning its coercive powers to wrong ends, becoming the servant of class, material interest, or national spirit. The body transforms these powers where they are, so that we can say that the church is also present where it transforms classes into mutually supporting, open opportunities to contribute to the whole, where it transforms individual contracts into corporate opportunities to serve the commonwealth, where it transforms ethnic groups into covenanted communities of mutuality and nurture, where it transforms the spirit of peoples into the common quest for shared principles of justice and virtue, and where it takes the wayward powers of philosophy and wealth, of the arts and the art of love, of technology and of nature, and turns them to the service and glory of God. As Noll points out, echoing Kuyper, the church provides a locus where Christ can stand in the midst of the people and teach them that all the other spheres are to be claimed by him also.

We should emphasize that this approach requires first of all a social theory of politics rather than a political theory of society. It also alters our understanding of how Christ relates to politics—through the ongoing and steady influence of the church on the society-forming forces rather than directly through seizing political power or merely through the attitudes of converted individuals. From this perspective, it is doubtful whether there is a distinctively Christian politics, although there certainly can be a public theology—a Christian theory of society rooted in ecclesiology—and thus a Christian philosophy of politics based on it. However, all of these—a social theory of politics, a public theology, and a Christian philosophy of politics—are mediated, so that when we move into politics, we must engage directly the wisdom of the political scientist and the politician. The main point is that the Christian engages politics first of all as a polity, and not in terms of specific policies. These can be worked out, more or less, in due course if we know something about the kind of society we want politics to sustain and defend.

The Relationship of Christ to Politics

This brings us to the relationship of Christ to politics. The main insight here is that the relationship is indirect, mediated through the church and its impact on society through ethics and the formation of moral strategies, platforms, and planks—to the extent we can persuade people that these are just. If the polity is open, pluralistic, and well structured, almost nothing prevents Christians from pursuing the policies they think they are called to pursue. This means that Christians have to persuade people to build the fabric of the many sectors of society from the inside out, and this entails drawing them into communities of worship in a polity that allows freedom of worship and the rights of religious groups to preach, teach, and organize on public matters.

What a difference it makes when a society has a church. The church's task is to help define the values that guide public policy, to illumine the deepest interests of society, to model in church polity the structures of authority implied by how we think God wants humans to live together, and to remind the people of God of their calling to live out the implications of these in the multiple spheres of life. When there is a church at the core of society, all of the institutions and functions of civilization are rearranged, and all of the bases for action that they identify are relativized. When a church is the center of loyalty and commitment, that which holds the various systems together has a ground in God, whom the peoples of the world partly know through the creation and possibly through the Holy Spirit. They tend to distort this principle of unity, however, unless they also know God through Jesus Christ and thus through all the Persons of the Trinity in community.

I am suggesting that we cannot deal adequately with the relationship of Christ to politics unless we not only take up the matters of systematic theology and the systematic understandings of society but also develop a profound and ultimately ecumenical sense of the church. On these bases, we may be able to develop an organized vision to guide the power of religion in the fabric of our increasingly cosmopolitan society. It may be that this vision is the most important way in which Christians relate to politics. This possibility suggests a need for a major qualification of the perspective set forth by Noll. Time after time when he turns to politics, Noll makes reference to the use of biblical images in debates over policies—Bryan's "cross of gold," Roosevelt's crusade against the corruption of political bosses by business, Julia Ward Howe's "Battle Hymn" for the Union against slavery, struggles against gambling, and the current battles over abortion. These are all important, but the most important debates may not be those over specific policies, but those that deal with the nature of the social order.

What about the cross then, which is Noll's way of calling for a certain humility in the face of political issues? I agree with the necessity of humility, but I think it might best come from the indirect way in which Christians work in politics—

allowing people to make up their own minds, being willing to listen to people's reservations, and seeking to address the objections of opponents—more than from a reluctance to speak with forthright confidence about moral and spiritual matters that we think are quite clear. In working with persons, of course, there is no substitute for a direct relationship. In relation to society, however, Christians have to work by the persuasive power of the word, by proclamation and argument, and by the slow influence of the church on all aspects of society rather than by the power of the political sword or of the threatened bloc votes if our policies are not adopted. It is not that the use of coercive force is altogether evil, but as to how and where force may legitimately be used in a pluralistic polity, even the most humble conviction and pious hope regarding its use must make the case before the courts of public opinion, jurisprudence, and scholarship that some policies, and not others, are warranted and just. This approach has the additional merit that it limits the kinds of triumphalism we have heard from the liberationist Left and the libertarian Right in recent years.

These debates best take place, in my view, before an empty cross. The Christ who guides the soul of believers as we think of both church and state is the resurrected Lord. The empty cross is the cross of triumph, of victory. It is the empty cross of Easter, not the crucifix of suffering, that is the center of the Protestant traditions shared by all parts of this family reunion. With our fellow Catholic Christians, we share a memory of the agony of Good Friday, and with our Orthodox friends, the cross with the extra, crooked bar, signifying on one side the unfinished pain of earthly suffering and on the other the lifted angle toward the ascension. Our central symbol, though, is the empty cross of Easter and Christ's triumphal victory over sin, death, and evil.

While I sometimes worry about the triumphalism of some Christians who speak on social and political issues, I am more worried about two other factors. One is the peril that I believe haunts the Kuyperian tradition. At its depth, this tradition is more deeply rooted in the Catholic, Reformational, civilization-forming, and genuinely ecumenical traditions of the church than in the sectarian, pietistic, communitarian, civilization-averting, and essentially evangelistic styles to which it has sometimes become attached, especially at the hands of migrants seeking to use theology to preserve ethnic identity against the cultures they encountered in such locations as South Africa and the United States. I am thus fearful of the tendencies that incline this great tradition to its weaker alliances in the faith.

The other concern is with the timidity with which most people speak of their faith as it relates to public issues beyond those of their personal convictions. I thus find in the symbol of the empty cross an assurance of courage and hope that I want to encourage in a public theology. On this point, at the foot of the cross understood in this way, I suspect that Noll and I are closer kin than it might seem at first glance.

Where Kingdom Politics Should Lead Us

Response by James W. Skillen

Mark Noll is properly concerned that Christians take their Lord, Jesus Christ, seriously. This means honoring the whole person and work of Christ, including his death on the cross. "If our entire apprehension of the world is shaped by our need of a savior," he states, "and if God offers himself as that savior, then the means by which God offers the savior should affect our apprehension of the entire world, including the world of politics." There could not be a more important starting point than this for the Kuyper Lecture, and the responses by James Bratt and Max Stackhouse give some indication of how many implications there are to Noll's thesis.

In these concluding reflections, I want not only to join the conversation with Noll and his respondents but also to point out some of the challenges that their comments pose for the Center for Public Justice. Insofar as the Center wants to take

James W. Skillen (Ph.D., Duke University) is Executive Director of the Center for Public Justice. Previously he taught politics at Messiah, Gordon, and Dordt colleges. He is the author of several works, including *The Scattered Voice: Christians at Odds in the Public Square* (Grand Rapids: Zondervan, 1990) and *Recharging the American Experiment: Principled Pluralism for Genuine Civic Community* (Grand Rapids: Baker, 1994).

seriously the confession that Christ is Lord, it must continually ask how its public policy research and civic education efforts should be conducted in the light of that confession. What may the Center learn from the preceding discussion?

The Cross and Triumphalism

Noll's most basic criticism of many so-called Christian political efforts appears to be that Christians have too often claimed the risen and triumphant Christ as their political champion or inspiration while ignoring the humility, self-sacrifice, and suffering of Christ's cross. The worst consequences of this appear when Christians, who are sinners saved by grace, claim that their own ideas, principles, or political power directly represent God's universal will, and on that basis they stand in a position of divine righteousness from which they may rightly subject all others to God's will. Noll is bold enough to say at one point that "a Christian politics that assumes a godlike stance toward the world is a Christian politics that has abandoned Christ."

Now the simplest and most direct way to answer this misguided triumphalism would seem to be by way of a correct interpretation of the relation between Christ's cross and his crown. Such an interpretation would have to relate the present age to the coming final judgment and to the fulfillment of God's kingdom in the day of the Lord. Noll comes very close to this when he says: "Christ indeed promises to appear in the last day with power and great glory, but only in the last day. In the interim, in anticipation of that last day, those who would be Christians are urged to take up their crosses and follow Jesus—not to victory, but to the denial of their own selves." If this is correct, then it would seem to follow that Noll identifies as legitimate the kind of Christian politics that grows from self-denial, that claims no special position or triumph for Christians in this age, and that waits patiently for Christ to exercise the authority of his crown in the last day. In other words, a truly Christian politics in this age should be cross-politics not crown-politics.

Noll does not go quite this far, however. He does not entirely reject a crown-politics in this age even though he has directly accused it of abandoning Christ. Somehow ruling and righteousness, which amount to more than self-denial, are essential to politics, he says, and this is due to the very character of our creatureliness and not only to our sinfulness. Christ is also the "creating Christ" and not only the "suffering Christ," Noll says. In other words, politics properly belongs to human creatures as a responsibility of ruling and enforcing justice, of governing and upholding righteousness. More than the cross must be at work here.

Cross and Crown in Tension?

The way Noll puts cross and crown together is by trying to hold them in tension with one another. At several points he says or implies that forms of triumphalism, even though they imply a godlike stance, are okay as long as they are balanced by an emphasis on the cross. Within basic biblical guidelines, he says, "the practicalities of a Christian politics alert to the cross may not differ all that much from a Christian politics inspired by the vision of the ruling Christ." Clearly, Noll does not want to abandon the "achievements gained by concentrating on creation and its restoration." In fact, Christians who "exploit the God-given realities of created political potential" may be able to do it even better "by seasoning images of Christ's ruling at the head of the saints over a restored creation with images of Christ's suffering for the saints on the cross."

Even this does not quite satisfy Noll, though, as he makes clear in referring to William Jennings Bryan's use of the language and images of the cross in his political speeches. As Noll points out, the "use of cross-language in the same militant manner as crown-language is far from uncommon in

Western history," so the mere seasoning of crown-imagery with cross-imagery is not sufficient to achieve what he wants. The question thus remains: What do the cross and crown of Christ have to do with earthly politics when understood in their proper interconnection?

It seems to me that Noll is too quick to place the cross of Christ in tension with a long-standing and admittedly mistaken appropriation of Christ's crown. He should, instead, reject that mistake and seek to recover the full and proper context of God's creating, judging, and redeeming purposes in Christ. In other words, Noll tries to use cross-language to fight misguided crown-language rather than to seek a recovery of the proper meaning and connection of both on biblical terms. Noll as well as Bratt leave standing—as crown-theology—the illegitimate tendency toward triumphalism and messianic self-righteousness on the part of Christians and then want to balance it by an opposite pole of self-abnegation and self-denial. Whether or not this is good Lutheranism, the consequence is that the cross itself ends up having little meaning for defining the actual structure and tasks of politics and is used by Noll in the end only to try to influence Christian attitudes. Noll's extended discussion of the particular versus the universal and of Lutheran dialectics does little to help us revise our conception of political order and civic responsibility.

Humility and the Meaning of Creation

Let me return to the meaning of creation for a moment. Noll admits that the Son of God is the "creating Christ"—the "Second Person of the Trinity, through whom and for whom all things were created in the beginning." Clearly, the biblical basis of humility is God's creation order, not the subsequent fact of human sinfulness. By their very nature, humans are not God and therefore have no grounds for thinking of themselves as God. Their godlikeness is always as the image of God, as dependents on God, as servants of God, as those called to walk in obedience to every word of the Lord. Any political responsibility that humans ever have in this world by virtue of God's good creation order thus should be exercised as humble service on the Creator's terms. We know from the Bible that the Creator's terms are those of justice, fair treatment, care of the poor, preserving life, and much more. Taking the creation and its restoration seriously does not provide a basis for Christians to put themselves in God's shoes or to imagine themselves to be the messianic judge or righteous master of the world. The Creator's terms for human politics rather should mean public service that upholds justice, insists on fair treatment, keeps the poor in special view, and preserves life. Insofar as the cross represents God's judgment against sin, it includes judgment against all political pretension that leads away from such service. The only way for humans to take Christ's crown seriously, then, is to see how Christ is *now* ruling the earth with patience and mercy, and to wait on God to fulfill the messianic promises made in and through Christ.

At present, as Noll affirms, Christ has called his disciples to follow him in service. This should mean recognizing not only that we are sinners in need of a savior but that the Savior is calling us back to the life of humble creatures and faithful stewards in God's creation. The trinitarian God is currently allowing rain and sunshine to fall on the just and unjust alike. We are supposed to be like our Father in heaven, thus we too should seek the well-being of our neighbor, including the unbelieving neighbor. Our Lord has not called us to clean the tares out of the wheat field; that will come in the end, on God's terms, and by other means. We are not the Messiah, and our states and political systems in this world are not the kingdom of God. Crown-politics, then, must be Christ's politics, and at present, allegiance to our king, Jesus Christ, does not mean that we should be trying to immanentize the eschaton or to complete the Messiah's work for him. It means seeking to promote justice in accord with the manner in which our King is now doing justice to all.

Should not then our allegiance to Christ—the Restorer of creation, the Judge of sin, and the Lord over all lords—mean seeking diligently to be public servants in the political arena? Every effort to do so, of course, should be done with full awareness that our motives may be impure, that our habits are distorted, and that our designs will be imperfect and not always just. Surely, however, political responsibility, like any other human responsibility, must go beyond the development of cautious and humble attitudes; it should work for real reforms of an unjust status quo. In a family, parents might fail to do properly and humbly what God calls parents to do, just as teachers or attorneys or doctors or pastors also might act selfishly and too self-righteously. All of this is the fruit of sin, but the proper response to these failures must not be merely to urge a sacrificial attitude. Beyond that we must ask, What kind of humble, self-sacrificing actions are appropriate for creatures in their various capacities—for citizens as citizens, for parents as parents, for teachers as teachers, and so forth? What does God require of us to reform the institutions of our lives so that we might serve God properly and humbly?

This is the point at which I think Noll and his respondents could do more with one of the most important contributions Christians have helped make to modern politics. Both in America and in Holland, and in other countries as well, Christians have finally given up the political error of believing that they alone have the right to hold citizenship and public office in the political order. They have, for the most part, relinquished what never was biblical but which had been absorbed thoroughly in different ways by Eastern and Western Christianity. The error grew from the Roman imperial conviction that divine order is mediated to the earth only through the emperor. The emperor thus came to be seen as the sole vicar of God on earth. When the emperor Constantine became a Christian, he tried to synthesize the two in an uncomfortable combination, and not until after the Reformation was this error rejected.

My point is that during the long development of Western politics, Christians have by and large moved from an imperialistic, church-dominated approach to politics to one in which they have come to recognize all citizens as equal by constitutional right under a limited government. In late nineteenth-century Holland, Abraham Kuyper led the way in rejecting even Calvin's lingering attachment to Christian imperialism, as Bratt points out. Kuyper, as did many North American Christians, fought for equal political rights, equal educational rights, and equal religious rights for all citizens.

It seems to me that this is one of many constructive Christian expressions of creation-order politics that has grown from repentance and humility at the foot of the cross and that requires an imitation of God's patience in not trying through human political power to complete God's final judgment. Even the most ardent right wing Christians in America today do not suggest that the United States government is the sole mediator between God and the world. In the spirit of both Noll and Bratt, we might of course ask why it took Christians so long to come to this position, and why so many Christians even today still do not have a well-developed doctrine of why this should be so.

Does the dire picture of American politics that Bratt paints suggest that a servant-politics is still far from the aspirations of most Christians? One reason why this may be difficult today is that too many Christians continue to see America through civil-religious glasses as God's specially chosen nation. They are willing to use both cross- and crown-language to describe the United States instead of confining that language to God's new nation: the multigenerational, worldwide church of Christ. Their civil-religious nationalism is what must be rejected by showing that God's new nation in Christ, the bride of Christ, will be satisfied with nothing less than the final revelation of God's kingdom, which cannot be achieved by human political means.

The proper political means in this age, in tune with God's coming kingdom, require recognition that Christ's crown-authority is presently being exercised in patience and with mercy toward all. Christ's crown does not exist in tension with his cross. Christ really is ruling now as servant, but the simple fact is that the full implications of both his cross and his crown have not yet been realized. Our political obedience must be built, then, on humble recognition that the final judgment and rectification of all creation—when the sheep and the goats are separated—is in God's hands, not in ours. In the meantime, by the power of the Holy Spirit, who now moves freely out across the earth because of Christ's death and resurrection, we must be willing to suffer affliction and even death rather than promote injustice that is incompatible with Christ's lordship.

God's Covenant in Christ

This brings into view another important ingredient of Christian political responsibility. Noll suggests that somehow the cross of Christ illustrates or manifests the "miraculous combination of the particular and the universal." He then associates the particular with specific, contingent circumstances, and the universal with "the general truths of the Christian revelation." This language, however, has nothing to do with the cross, with self-denial, suffering, humility, or sacrifice. It comes from the Platonic-Aristotelian tradition in which it represents an attempt to account for the nature of reality. In that sense, it is language that conflicts with creation-order language. Noll then associates Christian truth with the universal while connecting contingent circumstances with the particular. This does not make sense on biblical grounds, however. God's creatures, which in all of their particularity reveal God, cannot be set in tension with general truths of Christian revelation. The incarnation of Jesus Christ, moreover, is not an illustration or instantiation of a wider or higher duality called particular-universal; the Son of God is the one in and through whom God created all things and in whom all things are now sustained. Greek categories will not work even to explain the meaning of the incarnation, much less the meaning of the cross.

The biblical context in which incarnation, cross, crown, and politics need to be accounted for is that of the trinitarian God's covenantal actions and promises. This is a particular, unique narrative that moves from the beginning of creation to the fulfillment of all things in the revelation of God's glory. The beginning of all covenants is the bond God made with creation, which includes a seventh day of divine satisfaction and joy—the promise of a celebration of work well done, the divine sabbath rest. Following the original human disobedience, God comes again and again to particular chosen ones, in the particularity of historical circumstances, to make specific covenants of protection, special blessing, and promise.

When the Son of God took on flesh in Jesus Christ, it then became clear, as the author of the Book of Hebrews explains, that all preceding covenants were really grounded in God's particular, all-embracing covenant in Christ. Likewise, all earthly covenants reach their fulfillment through Christ's incarnation, death, resurrection, ascension, and return in glory. God's covenant in Christ is the final covenant, the covenant that opens the eternal sabbath to all who are in Christ (Hebrews 4). It thus allows for the Spirit of the trinitarian, sabbath communion to come in power—to convict the world of sin and to redeem a people for God by drawing many brothers and sisters to new life in Jesus, their elder brother (John 16). All the particular dealings of God with humans in history thus are grounded and come to fulfillment in God's particular dealings through Jesus Christ by the power of the Holy Spirit.

The cross of Christ represents God's judgment against the sin of the whole world. That cross must not be overlooked, as Noll is right to insist. We may not ignore the reality of sin, the reality of God's judgment against sin, and the reality of God's patience and mercy toward this world because of Christ's sacrifice. Politically speaking, however, that cross has no dialectical, equivocal, or ambiguous relation to the creation or to the crown of Christ. The cross is what seals the death of all contradictions against God and creation. Christ was crucified because he was willing to be the servant and not only the master (Philippians 2). Such humility reveals God to us; it does not contradict God's true nature. Humans must indeed die with Christ by faith, or they will die the second death under the final judgment. This cross, which is followed by the resurrection (two movements that must never be separated), achieves God's restoration of creation and makes possible the final triumph of Christ with his people, to the glory of God.

The final revelation of the creation's king, Jesus Christ, is indeed what Christians should be looking forward to and calling everyone on earth to anticipate. They need to do this, however, by recognizing that God's completed kingdom can no more be represented by one of our earthly political orders than our political machinations can be identified with the actions of the Messiah. We must recognize, moreover, that our politics ought to be grounded in precisely this creational humility. Politics, too, requires our confession of and repentance from public injustice and our exhibition of the patience of God who has put off the final judgment and is calling all people to repentance at the foot of the cross.

This means that we must recognize the special role God gave to Israel among the nations and the ways God used both Israel and other nations to judge and bless one another in anticipation of the full dawn of God's reign. Now, with the first coming of Christ, all authority in heaven and on earth has been placed in his hands. There can no longer be any empire, nation, or coalition of states that may rightfully claim special privilege under God, as if any of these could represent uniquely the covenanting God as Israel once did.

We should see every political entity not as an uncomfortable combination of contingency and universal truth, but rather as one among many political entities called by God in history to uphold justice on limited terms under the patient, long-suffering reign of Jesus Christ until the King returns to complete his work of rectification and reconciliation. In contrast to Stackhouse, I would stress that this connection between Christ and politics is very direct, even when not understood or recognized, and is not only indirect through the church.

Kingdom Politics

All of this should affect Christian attitudes toward politics, to be sure, but even more important, it should affect the very structure and design of politics, law, and the policies of government. Politics is about public service in God's creation, about governing a commons occupied by all citizens. This should mean, among other things, that Christians ought to be working, even to the point of willingly suffering death, for an open society, for equal justice for all citizens, for a constitutionally limited government, and for the overcoming of civil-religious confusion about America, or any other country, as God's chosen nation.

More important than Stackhouse's reflections on the Trinity, it seems to me, are his admonitions about a structurally diverse society. Part of what humility should mean for Christian politics is that we should bow before God's real intentions for creation. To do justice means to give each creature its due, which means giving each differentiated realm of creation its due. Humans are not simply individuals living as citizens under governments. They are family members, artists, scientists, engineers, teachers, and much more, active in the pursuit of numerous vocations fitting for God's creatures. Political humility means a constitutional political order that directly gives proper legal recognition to these spheres of society. How to achieve this through the best political and legal means is one of the central concerns of the Center for Public Justice.

If Christians ought to be seeking the well-being of others, including that of non-Christians, and protecting the rights of the disadvantaged, then Christian politics should mean working for precisely those purposes in appropriate ways. This is the proper expression of humility and self-denial in the political arena, and it has to do with how citizens should seek to structure and enforce laws in order to treat their civic neighbors as themselves. Christians should work at this task of establishing a just political order with the knowledge that final judgment and resurrection are in Christ's hands, and that a politics humbled by the cross is a politics that by the power of the Spirit serves a patient and merciful king.

Notes

Introduction

1. I am grateful to James Skillen for some of the wording in this paragraph, and also for many years of patient tutelage on the connections between Christianity and politics.

2. I am pleased to acknowledge inspiration from Robert Benne and Christa Klein as American Lutherans who are trying to express a distinctly Lutheran outlook on questions of public life; see, for example, Robert Benne, *The Paradoxical Vision: A Public Theology for the Twenty-First Century* (Minneapolis: Fortress, 1995). A sensitive discussion of some of the themes in my paper, addressed from the framework of Kuyperian theology, is John Bolt, "Creation and Cross: The Tension in Reformed Ethics," in John Bolt, *Christian and Reformed Today* (Jordan Station, Ontario: Paideia, 1984).

3. See, for example, James W. Skillen, "The Political Confusion of the Christian Coalition," *Christian Century* (August 30–September 6, 1995): 816–22.

4. See, for example, Richard John Neuhaus and Charles Colson, eds., *Evangelicals and Catholics Together* (Waco: Word, 1995).

5. The periodical *Christian Week* out of Winnipeg is an outstanding source of news and reflection on the religious dimensions of recent Canadian politics.

6. I hope that the exposition of these arguments carries its own conviction; they are also, however, an extension of historical and biblical reflections published earlier in *One Nation Under God? Christian Faith and Political Action in America* (San Francisco: Harper & Row, 1988); with George Marsden and Nathan Hatch, *The Search for Christian America*, rev. ed. (Colorado Springs: Helmers and Howard, 1989); "Introduction" in *Religion and American Politics* (New York: Oxford University Press, 1990); and *The Scandal of the Evangelical Mind* (Grand Rapids: Eerdmans, 1994).

Chapter 1: Christ and Christian Reflection on Politics

1. Of the vast amount of writing on such themes, one of the most pertinent essays for Calvinist thinkers is Merold Westphal, "A Reader's Guide to 'Reformed Epistemology,'" *Perspectives* (November 1992): 10–13.

2. Andrew Walls, "Africa and Christian Identity," in Wilbert R. Shenk, ed., *Mission Focus: Current Issues* (Scottdale, Pa.: Herald, 1980), 217.

91

3. Gabriel Fackre, "An Evangelical Megashift?" *Christian Century* (May 3, 1995): 485.

Chapter 2: Christology and the Practice of Politics

1. William Jennings Bryan, "Speech Concluding Debate on the Chicago Platform," in *The First Battle: The Story of the Campaign of 1896* (Chicago: W. B. Conkey, 1896), 206.

2. John Milton Cooper Jr., *The Warrior and the Priest: Woodrow Wilson and Theodore Roosevelt* (Cambridge: Harvard University Press, 1983), 161.

3. George M. Marsden, *New School Presbyterians and the American Evangelical Mind* (New Haven: Yale University Press, 1970), 182–84.

4. *The Economist* (18 March 1995): 27.

5. I have expanded on such themes in the chapter "The Bible in Politics" in *One Nation Under God?*

Chapter 3: Christian Attitudes toward Politics

1. James Nuechterlein, "Lutheran Blues," *First Things* 52 (April 1995): 12. Under Nuechterlein and Richard John Neuhaus, the journal *First Things* has become a vitally important forum advancing first-order consideration of issues at the intersection of religion and politics.

2. For a haunting account of the political dead-ends of a thoroughly Lutheran piety, see Ruth Rehmann, *Der Mann auf der Kanzel: Fragen an einen Vater* (Munich: Carl Hansler Verlag, 1979), a daughter's narrative of a pious Lutheran pastor's political immobilization in the crucible of modern German affairs.

3. C. K. Barrett, *Church, Ministry, and Sacraments in the New Testament* (Grand Rapids: Eerdmans, 1985), 78.

4. Philip S. Watson, *Let God Be God! An Interpretation of the Theology of Martin Luther* (Philadelphia: Fortress, 1970 [1947]) remains a powerful summary of Luther's Christ-centered theology of redemption.

5. Aleksandr Solzhenitsyn, *The Gulag Archipelago, 1918–1956,* trans. Thomas P. Whitney (New York: Harper & Row, 1974), 168.

Chapter 4: Christian Perspectives on Politics

1. Quoted in John Lukacs, *Confessions of an Original Sinner* (New York: Ticknor and Fields, 1990), 32n.

2. William E. Hull, "We Would See Jesus" [sermon on John 12:21], Occasional Papers of the Provost, Samford University (February 12, 1995), 10.

3. Lamin Sanneh, "Gospel and Culture: Ramifying Effects of Scriptural Translation," in Philip C. Stine, ed., *Bible Translation and the Spread of the Church: The Last 200 Years* (Leiden: E. J. Brill, 1990), 10–11.

4. Harro Höpfl, ed., *Luther and Calvin on Secular Authority* (New York: Cambridge University Press, 1991), x.

5. See Lewis W. Spitz, "Luther's Ecclesiology and His Concept of the Prince as *Notbischof,*" *Church History* 22 (1953): 113–41.

6. The meticulous notation by John T. McNeill of the editorial changes in the various versions of the *Institutes* makes this comparison possible; see John T. McNeill,

ed., *Calvin: Institutes of the Christian Religion*, trans. Ford Lewis Battles, 2 vols. (Philadelphia: Westminster Press, 1960).

7. Groen van Prinsterer, *Lectures on Unbelief and Revolution*, ed. Harry Van Dyke (Jordan Station, Ontario: Wedge, 1989), par. 149.

8. James W. Skillen, "The Kuyper Lecture," pamphlet from the Center for Public Justice (1995), 8.

9. Abraham Kuyper, *Lectures on Calvinism* (Grand Rapids: Eerdmans, 1931), 22, as quoted in Richard J. Mouw, "Lutherans from a Reformed Perspective," *Word & World* 11 (summer 1991): 301. Mouw's essay is superb on indicating how Lutheran and Calvinist strengths may be combined.

10. Frank Vandenberg, *Abraham Kuyper* (St. Catharines, Ontario: Paideia, 1978), 193–232. Vandenberg is not analytical about Kuyper's tenure as prime minister but does provide an outline of its course.

11. See the carefully qualified discussion in André du Toit, "Puritans in Africa? Afrikaner 'Calvinism' and Kuyperian Neo-Calvinism in Late Nineteenth-Century South Africa," *Comparative Studies in Society and History* 27 (1985): 227–30; and du Toit, "The Construction of Afrikaner Chosenness," in *Many Are Chosen: Divine Election & Western Nationalism*, eds. William R. Hutchison and Hartmut Lehmann (Minneapolis: Fortress, 1994), 126–29. I am grateful to Professor Mark Amstutz for pointing out the need for caution in making grand assertions about the use of Kuyper's ideas in South Africa.

Conclusion

1. Michael Novak, "A New Vision of Man: How Christianity Has Changed Political Economy," *Imprimis* [Hillsdale College] (May 1995): 7.

2. Abraham Kuyper, "Sphere Sovereignty," trans. Wayne A. Kobes in "Sphere Sovereignty and the University: Theological Foundations of Abraham Kuyper's View of the University and Its Role in Society" (Ph.D. dissertation, Florida State University, 1993), Appendix 3, p. 337. Originally published as *Souvereiniteit in Eigen Kring* (Amsterdam: J. H. Kruyt, 1880).

Response by James D. Bratt

1. Quoted in George Puchinger and Nicolaas Scheps, *Gesprek over de onbekende Kuyper* (Kampen: J. H. Kok, 1971), 63. Since Noll's paper raises the question of which type of cross we should add to crown, it is worth noting from pictorial evidence that Kuyper was referring to a large plaque depicting the entire crucifixion scene, including the criminals hanging on either side of Christ and people weeping beneath him. Kuyper purchased the piece already in his student days. See Jan de Bruijn, *Abraham Kuyper—leven en werk in beeld* (Amsterdam: Passage, 1987), 340.

2. Quoted in de Bruijn, *Abraham Kuyper*, 214.

3. See James D. Bratt, *Dutch Calvinism in Modern America: A History of a Conservative Subculture* (Grand Rapids: Eerdmans, 1984), 67–72.

4. Ibid., 97, 260.

5. Kuyper's classic conversion narrative is in *Confidentie* (Amsterdam: Hoeveker, 1873).

6. See James D. Bratt, "John W. Nevin and the Antebellum Culture Wars," in Arie Griffioen and Sam Hamstra Jr., eds., *John Williamson Nevin: A Collection of Essays* (Metuchen, N.J.: Scarecrow Press, 1996).

7. Abraham Kuyper, *Lectures on Calvinism* (Grand Rapids: Eerdmans, 1931), 139–41.

8. Peter Heslam, "Abraham Kuyper's Lectures on Calvinism" (D.Phil. thesis, Oxford University, 1993), 125.

Response by Max L. Stackhouse

1. See, for example, José Casanova, *Public Religions in the Modern World* (Chicago: University of Chicago Press, 1994); Peter van der Veer, *Religious Nationalism* (Berkeley: University of California Press, 1994); and Mark Juergensmeyer, *The New Cold War?* (Berkeley: University of California Press, 1993).

2. These are major themes in my *Christian Social Ethics in a Global Era*, with Peter Berger, Dennis McCann et al. (Nashville: Abingdon Press, 1995). Many implications for domestic life are also present in Stanley W. Carlson-Thies and James Skillen, eds., *Welfare in America: Christian Perspectives on a Policy in Crisis* (Grand Rapids: Eerdmans, 1995), and for international life, in George Weigel, ed., *A New Worldly Order* (Washington: Ethics and Public Policy Center, 1992).

3. See M. H. Abrams, *Natural Supernaturalism* (New York: Norton, 1971).

4. Noll does not fully treat in this address the kingdom ideas he wants to modulate, but if he has in mind the several adaptations of kingdom themes treated in H. Richard Niebuhr, *The Kingdom of God in America* (New York: Harper & Row, 1937), he would have to recognize that the evangelical "reign of Christ" is already a part of the triune kingdom themes, which include also the Puritan "sovereignty of God" and the Social Gospel "coming kingdom" ideas.

5. See John Bolt, *Calvinist Trinitarianism and Theocentric Politics* (Toronto: Edwin Mellin Press, 1989); and A. Ganoczy, "Observations on Calvin's Trinitarian Doctrine of Grace," in E. A. McKee et al. eds., *Probing the Reformed Tradition* (Louisville: Westminster/John Knox Press, 1989).

6. I think much contemporary theology is too influenced by Karl Barth's Christocentrism on one side and the Anabaptist's Jesusolatry on the other. I find Reinhold Niebuhr's "Where Christ Is and Is Not Expected" in *Nature and Destiny*, vol. 2 (New York: Scribner & Sons, 1939) a more compelling and authentically evangelical treatment of the larger biblical context, one fully in accord with later trinitarian developments.

7. I have in mind the tragic turn of many pastors to the sectarianism of Stanley Hauerwas, William Willimon, and John Howard Yoder. For a good contrast, see Glen Tinder, *The Political Meaning of Christianity* (Baton Rouge: Louisiana State University Press, 1989).

8. This matter has long concerned me and, with matters of anthropology, eschatology, and ecclesiology, stands at the core of theology in my view. See, for example, "The Trinity as Public Theology," in Mark Heim, ed., *From Faith to Creed* (Grand Rapids: Eerdmans, 1991), 162–97.

9. I have elsewhere argued that this is one of the key turning points of Western civilization, one that made it possible for Christianity to transcend its Hebraic and Hellenistic context, and one that both evangelicals and liberals ought to take more

seriously. See *Ethics and the Urban Ethos* (Boston: Beacon Press, 1973; reprint edition forthcoming).

10. An enormous amount of scholarly work has been done on the Crusades since the Enlightenment, when it was regularly argued that religion, and specifically Christianity, was the cause of war, an idea that, oddly, is shared by many evangelicals who otherwise oppose many of the assumptions of the Enlightenment. See Jonathan Riley-Smith, *The Oxford Illustrated History of the Crusades* (New York: Oxford University Press, 1995); and "The Crusades," *Christian History*, vol. XII, no. 4 (issue 40, 1993). It was among the chief insights of Kuyper that he recognized that militant violence derived more from the secular ideologies of revolution that repudiated Christianity than from Christian influence. In America the debate over the faith as a cause of violence remains unsettled, with some seeing Columbus and the settlers as typical models of imperialist conquest in the name of Christ, and others seeing the Puritans and frontier evangelists as the source of civility, taming the wilderness of the land and the human heart by establishing a pluralist, democratic society.

11. A series of papers on covenant, now being edited by Douglas Ottati and Douglas Schuurman, with extensive reference to these matters and their political implications, is forthcoming in the *Annual of the Society of Christian Ethics*, 1996.

12. See Daniel Elazar, *Covenant and Polity* (New Brunswick, N.J.: Transaction Books, 1994).

13. The American character is stamped by a profound interplay of Protestant and liberal thought that resists established doctrine. Part of this surely derives from the quest for religious freedom in America, but part of it may come from a denial of the fact that the concrete possibilities of religious freedom are dependent on the establishment of some, and not other, theologically based foundations.

14. See, for example, Adam Seligman, *The Idea of Civil Society* (New York: The Free Press, 1992); Herman Dooyeweerd, *A Christian Theory of Social Institutions*, trans. Magnus Verbrugge, ed. John Witte Jr. (La Jolla, Calif.: The Dooyeweerd Foundation, 1986); Conrad Cherry and Robert A. Sherrill, eds., *Religion, the Independent Sector, and American Culture; AAR Studies in Religion 63* (Atlanta: Scholars Press, 1992); Michael Walzer, *Spheres of Justice* (New York: Basic Books, 1983); and John F. A. Taylor, *The Masks of Society: An Inquiry into the Covenants of Civilization* (New York: Appleton-Century-Crofts, 1966).

Mark A. Noll is the McManis Professor of Christian Thought and professor of history at Wheaton College, where he has taught since 1979. He was educated at Wheaton (B.A., English), the University of Iowa (M.A., comparative literature), Trinity Evangelical Divinity School (M.A., church history), and Vanderbilt University (Ph.D., American religious history). He is a member of several professional societies, including the American Society of Church History and the conference on Faith and History.

Noll's main academic interests focus on the interaction of Christianity and culture in eighteenth- and nineteenth-century Anglo-American societies. He has authored or edited over a dozen books, including *Between Faith and Criticism: Evangelicals, Scholarship, and the Bible in America* (Grand Rapids: Baker, 1986, 2d ed. 1991), *A History of Christianity in the United States and Canada* (Grand Rapids: Eerdmans, 1992), *One Nation Under God? Christian Faith and Political Action in America* (New York: Harper & Row, 1988), *Religion and American Politics* (New York: Oxford University Press, 1989), and *The Scandal of the Evangelical Mind* (Grand Rapids: Eerdmans, 1994). With Nathan Hatch, he edits the Library of Religious Biography series published by Eerdmans. Noll's essays and reviews have appeared in a number of academic and popular journals.